ONTARIO
HOUSE STYLES

The distinctive architecture of the province's 18th and 19th century homes

ONTARIO
HOUSE STYLES

The distinctive architecture of the province's 18th and 19th century homes

ROBERT MIKEL

JAMES LORIMER & COMPANY LTD., PUBLISHERS
TORONTO

James Lorimer & Company Ltd. acknowledges the support of the Department of Canadian Heritage and the Ontario Arts Council in the development of writing and publishing in Canada. We acknowledge the support of the Government of Canada through the Book Publishing Industry Development Program (BPIDP) for our publishing activities. We acknowledge the support of the Government of Ontario through the Ontario Media Development Corporation's Ontario Book Initiative. We acknowledge the support of the Canada Council for the Arts for our publishing program.

Le Conseil des Arts | The Canada Council
du Canada | for the Arts

ONTARIO ARTS COUNCIL
CONSEIL DES ARTS DE L'ONTARIO

page 2: *An unusual five-bay Ontario Cottage with original incised stucco made to resemble stone — Paris, Ontario.*

Photo credits:
Legend: T — top; C — center; R — right; L — left; B — bottom

Jack Chiang: 11, 20, 24, 42R, 47, 48BL, 48BC, 66, 71R, 74, 78L, 81R, 81CR, 87, 93, 102
Dwayne Coon: 3, 5, 14, 15, 16, 18TC, 18BC, 18R, 22, 23, 25, 30, 31, 38, 39, 44T, 44BL, 44BC, 45, 50, 53R, 54, 63, 68, 69, 76, 77, 85, 86, 94, 99TR, 99B, 109C, 109TR, 109BR, 114, 116R, 117, 118, 119, 121, 124L, 125, 126R
Terry Manzo: 8, 9, 10, 12, 15L, 17, 18L, 19, 28, 32L, 32C, 35, 36, 40R, 41, 44BR, 48TR, 48TC, 55, 59, 60, 64, 67, 70, 71BL, 71C, 72, 73, 78R, 79, 80R, 81TL, 81BL, 89TR, 89BR, 90, 96, 97, 98, 99L, 107, 108B, 109TL, 109BL, 110, 112R, 113, 115, 116TL, 116BL, 122, 124R
Vincenzo Pietropaolo: 6, 26, 27, 32R, 33, 34, 40L, 40C, 42L, 42C, 43, 46, 49, 52, 53L, 56, 57, 58, 62, 82, 84, 88, 89TL, 89C, 89BL, 92, 95, 100, 103, 104, 105, 106, 108T, 108L, 112T, 112L, 112C, 123

Library and Archives Canada Cataloguing in Publication

Mikel, Robert, 1956-

    Ontario house styles : the distinctive architecture of the province's 18th and 19th century homes / Robert Mikel.

Includes bibliographical references and index.

ISBN 1-55028-845-8 (pbk.)

    1. Architecture, Domestic—Ontario—History—18th century. 2. Architecture, Domestic—Ontario—History—19th century. 3. Historic buildings—Ontario. I. Title.

NA7242.O5M44 2004   728'.09713   C2004-903852-4

James Lorimer & Company Ltd., Publishers
35 Britain Street
Toronto, Ontario
M5A 1R7
www.lorimer.ca

Printed and bound in Canada

Acknowledgements

I am very grateful to James Lorimer for providing me the opportunity to work on such an interesting project, and for the guidance, input, and perseverance of editors Kristen Pederson Chew, Frank Edwards, and Chad Fraser.

My thanks to Lisa Roberts, Sandra Black, Michael McClelland, Edward Boudreau, Dustin Parkes, and Al Kenny, who all in various ways supported and contributed to creation of this book. A very heartfelt thanks in particular to Margaret Baily, whose advice, research, support, and participation were invaluable. Margaret's keen interest, in-depth knowledge, and commitment to preserving Ontario's heritage are inspiring. I would also like to thank Colonel and Mrs. Norman Allen for all the kind support and encouragement they have given me over the years. A special tribute to my very much missed late parents, who gave me so many opportunities and advantages in life.

There are ample resources available on Ontario's historical architecture for anyone interested in exploring this topic further. Books, local libraries, municipalities, heritage organizations, and Web sites abound. I have drawn on many of them, and I appreciate the efforts of all those who have contributed to the study of Ontario's past.

Finally, this book would not have been possible without the cooperation of the many property owners who allowed their houses to be profiled in this book. The pride and responsible stewardship of homeowners such as these help to safeguard our valuable heritage for many years to come.

— R.M.

Contents

Introduction

Diversity is the most outstanding feature of architectural style in rural and urban Ontario. Drive through any part of the province, and you are apt to find a treasure trove of house styles — from Georgian manors to Craftsman bungalows.

The province was founded on the cusp of one of the greatest periods of economic, political and social change the western world has ever witnessed. Industrialization exploded onto the nineteenth-century stage with a burst of ideas, technological innovations and scientific discoveries that created both political and social upheaval, but also great wealth. Nationalism grew, and the landed- and middle-classes expanded and flourished. This resulted in an explosion of the arts, as the kaleidoscope of these influences found physical expression, most visibly in architecture.

Architecture is much more than a decorative style that can be identified by a series of elements. It is an expression of the social beliefs, ideas and cultural philosophies of any given society at a particular time. Even Ontario's first Loyalist settlers understood this. Once they could afford to build more substantial houses, they chose the Georgian style,

Wonderful and rare trompe l'oeil *decoration found in Castle Kilbride near Waterloo.*

which to them represented tradition and elegance, and physically expressed their connection to England. From 1784 to the outbreak of World War I, Ontario saw no less than twelve architectural styles come and go. Considering that western architecture had evolved very slowly over the previous 500 years, the variety of architecture by the turn of the century must have been striking. Styles came in rapid succession, and often coexisted for years. As a result, these styles were often mixed. There was also a strong desire to improve, modernize, and enlarge houses according to current trends, causing styles to be grafted to earlier forms. There are purer expressions of certain styles, but the majority of Ontario houses exhibit more than one stylistic influence.

There are, however, several common general trends that affected all Ontario house styles. Technological developments gave greater structural freedom, so houses could be larger with more rooms and space; ceilings grew taller, which in turn made houses higher. As decorative features became cheaper, they became more popular and more common; flat Georgian surfaces became more three-dimensional, windows and doors were recessed into walls, their decorative elements, like sills and window heads, more decorated and prominent. Porches, bay windows, towers, turrets, verandahs, and belvederes were added to the exterior to enliven the composition. These were often embellished with strong decorative details and occasionally with bold colour. Compare a Georgian window with a later Italianate and the difference is clear — the former is square and plain, the latter much longer with more decorated trim. Or compare early porches or verandahs to later ones, no matter what the style, and you will see that later Victorian porches are generally highly decorated and early porches simpler. Part of this trend comes from the desire of new and growing conservative middle classes to display their newfound wealth. The trend of historicism comes from these same impulses. Historical revivals, while new and different, also by their pedigrees and recognizable symbols represented tradition, stability, and safety.

Towards the end of the nineteenth century, through the Arts and Crafts and Queen Anne

Elaborate Italianate treatment of the bay window and front entrance.

Georgian windows — squarish and plain. Victorian windows tended to be elongated and more highly decorated.

styles, attempts were made to evolve a modern architecture, but for the most part nineteenth-century homes remained conservative. At the beginning of the twentieth century, however, there was a tremendous reaction against the excesses of the Victorian age and desire to return to simpler times. The result was Georgian, colonial, and Tudor houses infused, of course, with all modern creature comforts. These conservative house styles remain popular today.

Yet the conservative casings of the nineteenth century mask some very revolutionary changes. Followers of the Romantic movement, for example, believed that one's surroundings should stimulate and championed naturalistic landscapes, leading to a revolutionary way of looking at the outdoors. Up to this time, nature was viewed as a force to be tamed, and landscapes were formal, structured extensions of the house. The Romantic movement led to naturalized landscapes and eventually to the evolution of the lawns and gardens that are familiar to us today. In Ontario, where the wilderness was still being settled, this had particular resonance. It also changed the relationship between a house and its surroundings, as the two became increasingly integrated.

This concept was further developed during the Gothic revival, and the idea that the physical form of a house should be a function of its plan. This organic approach had a profound impact. The ideal Georgian house was completely symmetrical, both in plan and in elevation. Rooms with different functions were identical. The Georgian house represented good taste and breeding, so while it was not practical for Ontario houses to conform this closely to the Georgian ideal, Georgian principles were still vigourously applied. This changed in the province during the 1860s, when asymmetrical designs became more popular, as the principles of the Romantic movement found full expression in the eclecticism of the Queen Anne house.

The idea of the house as a cozy place also illustrates the tremendous change that occurred in home design from the late Georgian period to 1914. In medieval times, the workplace and residence were often combined, and in many cases a number of people lived in the house, which resulted in very little privacy and personal comfort. By the end of the Georgian era, the workplace and the home had for the most part separated. As industrialization progressed, the house was increasingly seen as a refuge from the world and a place of comfort. It also increasingly became the purview of women, as men became increasingly absent. In the eighteenth century, house decoration was largely a man's job. This changed during the nineteenth century, and a cult of domesticity sprang up that had a profound effect on the role of women, whose main responsibility became making the home a place of sanctuary for her husband and children.

House plans became increasingly complex at this time as well. The four-room Georgian was no longer sufficient for the needs of a prosperous Victorian. Houses could include a study, library, music room, ballroom, conservatory, parlour, drawing room, dining room, or breakfast room. The bedrooms were separated from the living areas, and often possessed an adjoining dressing room. The increasing staff necessary to run such establishments were located as far away from the living spaces as possible, in a complex series of kitchens, pantries, sculleries and laundry areas. Such complex plans were vanquished by the return of simpler houses at the turn of the century.

Ontario's early houses are an important part of our history, architectural tradition, and physical environment. They embody the personal side of our history: the most visible legacy of those individuals and families who built this province. And what a legacy it is — a rich staple of interesting, eccentric, and beautiful dwellings that reflect social and cultural circumstance as well as individual aspirations. This heritage needs to be preserved. This book is intended to foster further interest in, and love for, Ontario's rich architectural heritage.

An ornate Queen Anne house in Brockville with American Stick treatment.

Georgian Architecture

1784-1860

England's emergence as a world power early in the eighteenth century coincided with the ascension of the Teutonic Hanovers to the English throne. After the death in 1714 of Queen Anne, the last Stuart monarch, the crown of England passed to the closest living Protestant heir, the Elector of Hanover, a great-grandson of James I, who became George I. He and his three successive heirs, all Georges, gave this period of British history, 1714–1830, its name.

During the Georgian period, England enjoyed one of its longest runs of political stability and economic growth. London emerged as Europe's financial capital, the royal navy came to dominate the seven seas, and the British empire rapidly expanded. The eighteenth century also saw the consolidation of power in the House of Commons under the leadership of Sir Robert Walpole, the first British prime minister in the modern sense, and the emergence of a large and wealthy middle class. English confidence and nationalism grew. It was the Age of Enlightenment, a time of ideas and energy, and a flourishing of political, economic, scientific, and artistic thought. The movement's followers lauded reason and individualism, and eschewed the excesses of the baroque period, which were associated with the Stuarts.

In architectural terms, England embraced neo-Palladianism. It was this architectural style that dominated the first half of the Georgian period, until about 1760, and is most identified with Georgian architecture. It was based on the architecture of Andrea Palladio

John Wissler House, a late Georgian dwelling displaying the style's simplicity, proportion, and symmetry.

(1508–1580), an architect who tried to recreate the style and proportions of the buildings of Ancient Rome in sixteenth-century Italy. Although neo-Palladianism was a continuation of the English classical renaissance, it was a much simpler and stricter interpretation of classical proportions than the baroque style it succeeded. Neo-Palladianism characterized much of Georgian architecture, with its stripped-down decoration, understated elegance, grace, and a formalized system of proportions that could be applied to the humble or grand, the public or private. It very much became a national architecture for all classes. It was free of the continental European, Catholic, and absolutist elements of the baroque from which the English were deliberately distancing themselves after the Glorious Revolution that deposed James II.

The Georgian style had a profound influence on England's emerging North American colonies. It brought architectural unity to a disparate group of colonies, as their inhabitants sought to emulate the mother country's fashions. Regional difference still existed, particularly between the eastern seaboard, the south, and the west. It was these regional colonial Georgian styles that the first settlers brought to Ontario.

The first permanent structures in Upper Canada were erected by these former residents of the Thirteen Colonies who had backed the losing side, Britain, during the American Revolution. Almost 10,000 English-speaking Loyalists landed in Ontario in 1784. At the time, the land was part of the recently acquired British colony of Quebec. Not wishing to be dominated by a French majority, the new inhabitants demanded a measure of self-rule, which led to the Constitutional Act of 1791, which created the provinces of Lower Canada (Quebec) and

Built circa 1808, the Field House in Niagara-on-the-Lake survived, though not unscathed, the War of 1812.

Upper Canada (Ontario). Having left their properties and much of their wealth behind, the loyalists were given land grants by the British government upon their arrival. Their first homes were made of logs but the Loyalists were soon able to build more substantial residences, the wealthier among them building quite sophisticated ones. Not surprisingly, they built in the Georgian style, which not only was familiar and comfortable to

Storm doors were added to protect expensive panelled ones from harsh weather.

them but demonstrated their patriotism and loyalty to the British crown. Those with limited funds followed with simpler houses, but the flexibility of the Georgian style meant it could be scaled to any budget.

The craftsmen who built these early houses were skilled and known for careful workmanship, but they were not innovative, and any modifications to the design of a house built in this pleasing but conservative style were left to the client's own dictates. Pattern books giving details associated with this style were readily available in the United States and from thence across the border to Upper Canada, so builders needing guidance could consult them to resolve design problems.

Georgian design was uncluttered, based on the rules of symmetry, proportion, and balance. The John Field House, near Niagara-on-the-Lake, is a handsome surviving example of an early design. Its solidly rectangular form with the front door on the long side of the house has a more gently sloping roof than was typical of a gable-end roof, and a plain wood eave cornice fits snugly to the house. Its massive unadorned chimneys, balanced on the end walls, complete the composition. The pleasing symmetrical façade, with rather small windows in relation to the brick surface typical of the period, is formally arranged with the same number of windows on either side of a central entrance. The central entrance is flanked by two windows on either side, with five running along the second floor. Each of the double-hung windows has a plain wooden window sill and no decorative surround. Each ground floor window has twelve-over-twelve panes while the upper floor has

The eave return, or returning eave: an attractive way to finish the cornice.

One-and-a-half-storey houses were popular because an extra floor could be added in the attic without increased taxation.

twelve-over-eight. The front door, which leads to a central hall is equally unadorned, with no decorative doorcase or transom, and a very modest sidelight to either side. The only decorative outburst comes from the porch, which has a broken pedimented roof supported by very slender columns and pilasters whose character is more neo-classical than Georgian. The Georgian design strove for a sense of solidity and decorum. Displays of the fanciful or idiosyncratic would have been seen as bad taste, again a reaction against baroque excesses.

Not all settlers had the means to build such a comfortable and commodious house as this. Houses could be anywhere from one storey to two and a half, made of clapboard, brick, or stone. The pitch of the roof was often steep, probably to deal with the Ontario winter snows. This neat clapboard house in Paris, Ontario, represents one of the most common forms of Georgian houses built in the province. It is a small, one-and-a-half-storey cottage, with a central transomed door flanked by small windows on either side; Georgian rules of proportion and symmetry still apply. This example has returning eaves and sits on a good stone basement, no doubt where the original kitchen was once

located. No expensive details adorn this compact cottage. The two-over-two paned windows probably replaced a multi-paned sash. However, the windows retain the squarish proportions favoured by the Georgians.

A slightly more elaborate house is the 1816 Miller House in Niagara-on-the-Lake, a town that boasts some of the most beautiful early buildings in the province. Mr. Miller was a very active fellow in town having been the coroner, registrar, county clerk, inspector and deputy clerk of the crown. The home is a simple storey-and-a-half gable form house of clapboard with massive end chimneys containing the stacks of seven chimneys. Fireplaces were the only source of heat; they were large and situated on external walls on

The simplest Georgian house form is the compact three-bay (opening) façade. The porch dates from the turn of the century. This home is located in Paris.

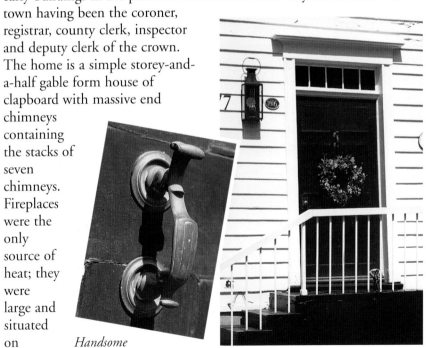

Handsome surviving early door knocker.

Early Georgian door with a five-pane transom and typical six-panelled door.

Traditional Georgian double-hung sash windows with twelve-over-twelve panes.

the short sides of the rectangle, thereby able to heat as many rooms as possible, though the centre hall would be rather chilly. Its façade is typical, with five openings, or bays, the central one being a plain doorway with a single sash window transom above. The front door has six panels, also typical of the style. Usually, as is the case here, two windows were placed proportionally on either side of the centre door. Since glass had to be shipped from afar and breakage was common, most panes were no larger than 7 x 8 inches, held in place by slender moulded wooden muntin bars. Glass was also subject to taxation, another deterrent to its use. Twelve panes over twelve panes, then, was the most commonly used pattern on larger windows. There is very little exterior trim — a simple moulded cornice with returning eaves and narrow flat corner boards. The roof sits rather high on the building, allowing for a generous half-storey, housing bedrooms.

Not all buildings conformed to the strict Georgian rules. Depending on circumstances and cultural backgrounds, variations appeared in the overall Georgian design. In Dundas, where a good number of Georgian houses survive, a local asymmetrical design was used. This Hait Street house shows all the characteristic Georgian features, but the arrangement of the windows is asymmetrical, with the front door flanked by two windows on one side and only one on the other. The

Above: An asymmetrical Georgian cottage, Dundas.

Left: Well-crafted stone masonry.

façade is cut stone in a regular pattern with single stone lintels and sills.

The Brubacher House, located on the campus of the University of Waterloo, is an interesting 1850 Pennsylvania German example of the Georgian style. After the American Revolution, many Mennonites left the hills of southern Pennsylvania for the lure of cheap land in southwestern Ontario. John and Magdelana Brubacher chose the gentle brow of a hill to build this typical and practical stone Pennsylvania German farmhouse, probably intending to recreate the environs of their

*Above: Farmhouse with
Pennsylvanian German influences.*

native state. Here they raised
their fourteen children in a house
that flatly refused to aspire to
British pretension. While the
house follows the Georgian form,
none of the structure's façades are
alike. The main façade faces north
and is asymmetrical with only four
bays, an off-centre eight-panelled
front door with two windows to one
side and only one on the other. Three windows running along the
second floor don't quite align with their first-floor counterparts. On the
south face, a plain-Jane verandah spans the front, while the basement is

*Above: River access usually meant plenty of
stone for building construction, as was the
case with this striking Paris terrace.*

cut away under the entrance for
purely functional reasons. Yet the
whole composition, with its crisp
white trim, has an attractive
utilitarian charm.

Row, or terrace, houses were
introduced early into Ontario,
anticipating rather than fulfilling
the need for higher density urban
housing. In Paris, Ontario, this handsome circa-
1850 terrace, with dressed sills, functioned as a hotel for a time. The
only embellishment is found in the treatment of the recessed doorways,
all treated slightly differently, two with full transoms and sidelights tied
together by delicate pilasters and wooden mouldings.

While the doors and windows are unusual for not having a regular,
if not symmetrical arrangement on the smooth-cut stone façade, the

A doorcase with Greek revival influence on the Paris terrace.

Above centre: The end parapet walls indicate the original owners of this simple five-bay Georgian home expected to have close neighbours.

Above right: A simple, unadorned Georgian entrance.

solid massing and form are decidedly Georgian. Fire was an all-too-common tragedy in early Ontario, and one can see the builder's concern about this hazard in the pair-chimney parapet wall rising between the two parts of the terrace. The wall provided a solid barrier between town houses as a means to stop fires from spreading between their roofs, which were then mostly made of wood. In an economical move the builder constructed the other less important façades of rubble stone and brick.

When buildings with parapet walls are found in isolation, it no doubt means the builder envisioned a time when the area around it would be highly built-up. An example of this is a charming single-storey brick house in Dundas. Here, parapet walls rising slightly above the roofline flank the five-bay symmetrical façade. Located on an early prominent road, one can see how the builder was protecting his house, anticipating that the area would eventually develop. That didn't occur, however, and a

Window details, Wissler House.

later owner added windows on the north face. This neat cottage is an excellent example of a later Georgian house with a front door with a transom light, chunky paired chimneys, shallow eave cornice, and overall good proportions.

However, many more affluent Ontarians continued to build solid two-storey brick five-bay residences well after the Georgian style had reached its peak. John Wissler's 1842 house in Waterloo illustrates the tenacity of the style. With the neo-classical, Regency, and Greek Revival in vogue, Wissler built himself a standard Georgian house with a well-balanced symmetrical façade with twelve-over-twelve windows, paired chimneys. It features little external detail with the exception of the plain eave cornice with eave returns, a raised banding course dividing the upper and lower floors, and the front door, which is recessed with a panelled reveal. This quintessentially English house owes much to the Dutch. After the Glorious Revolution of 1688, when the Dutch William of Orange and his wife Mary crossed the English Channel to rid England of the Papist James II and assume Britain's throne, he brought from his homeland architectural traits that were quickly assimilated into the British vocabulary. Double-hung windows, crisp, white-painted trim, red-brick and Flemish-bond brickwork (where alternating courses of half-brick and full-brick form the walls) were all introduced into England by William and Mary.

Top: In the Georgian period, chimneys were generally balanced on the end walls. Left: The door panels match the pattern on the covering of the doorway's reveal. Above: Wissler House, moulded chimney.

The Neo-Classical Style

1815-1850

The exciting discoveries of the Roman sites of Pompeii and Herculaneum at the base of Mount Vesuvius in the mid 1700s rekindled European interest in Ancient Rome. Rather than looking to the Renaissance's interpretations of the classical for inspiration, Europeans could now go directly to the source, which offered them a new richness of classical options.

The British architect Robert Adam and his brother James travelled to Italy taking notes and making sketches, and detailed drawings of ancient Roman sites. They published their observations in a three-volume work called *Works in Architecture*. Their designs adapted Roman features they had sketched and measured first-hand at the ruins, and they emulated the classical style rather than slavishly copying it. Political opponents of Sir Robert Walpole took up this new style in their challenge of the existing order, which they felt was embodied by the more rigid neo-Palladian style. Compared to the houses of the earlier Georgian style, these new ones looked lighter and offered a more refined version of classical features, now reinterpreted to adapt Roman architectural orders, forms, and decorative detail in less rigid ways. The effect was less solemn, more playful and lighthearted than the traditional Georgian form. Because the decor was based on ancient classical models, this new style became known as neo-classical, but it retained the symmetrical rules of the older Georgian style.

In France it became known as the Empire style and reached its

Macpherson House in Napanee. The Georgian façade became lighter and more elegant under the influence of the neo-classical.

zenith there under the reign of Napoleon. However, it was in the newly created United States that the style was embraced not just for aesthetic reasons but for political ones. Young American patriots eagerly adopted the powerful architectural style they believed represented the republican ideals of the new nation. Known in the United States as the Federal style, and later infused with Greek influences, one of its first proponents was Thomas Jefferson, whose designs for his own house, Monticello, and that of the University of Virginia introduced the style to his countrymen. In America, Asher Benjamin's pattern book *The Country Builder's Assistant* helped to popularize neo-classical designs.

Most builders in Upper Canada gleaned their ideas from pattern books, which themselves were based on the works of Adam or Benjamin. Builders blended and mixed decorative features with older Georgian forms. The neo-classic style is often called the Loyalist style, acknowledging the origins of those who populated the skylines of many Ontario communities.

During the War of 1812, while Britain was occupied with fighting in Napoleonic France, Americans tried unsuccessfully to invade Britain's newest colony, galvanizing settlers already in Upper Canada to be more British-loving than ever. The war had caused the destruction of many of the earliest Georgian houses, especially in the Niagara area, in Little York (Toronto), and along the Great Lakes and St. Lawrence River shoreline, so there was a great need for new construction all over Upper Canada.

Although the neo-classic had come to embody the ideals of the United States, this did not deter the second generation of Loyalists from embracing it. Their enthusiasm is a witness to the international importance of the style. In the minds of the Upper Canadians, it was much more than an American fashion.

The Niagara area suffered tremendously from the ravages of the war. In the colony's former capital, the bustling Newark, renamed Niagara-on-the-Lake, only two houses were left standing. In rebuilding, the citizens made much use of the neo-classical, and today this small town probably contains the highest concentration of neo-classical houses in the province.

The most noticeable change from the Georgian style is the treatment of the central entrance. It became a much more prominent element on the façade, wider than before, with an elliptical fan-shaped or flat transom, sidelights and door, all integrated into one eye-catching feature. The Georgian favoured the semi-circle, while the neo-classicist preferred the ellipse.

The importance of the door can be seen in the Breakenridge House, Niagara-on-the-Lake. Its magnificent entranceway, with its exaggerated fanlight set in a wide plain entablature with hood mould, is supported by stylized fluted Ionic pilasters framing the central six-panelled door giving the entrance much more drama. The fanlight and sidelights are

Breakenridge House.

Delicate and intricate detail are trademarks of the neo-classical.

filled with lacelike tracery. The whole has much more dimension and depth than earlier doorways and the proportions are thin relative to the dimensions of the whole building. The symmetrical Georgian form is decorated with Ionic pilasters, which rise two storeys to support the dentiled cornice entablature, which wraps around the clapboard building enclosing the gable ends to form pediments. The French windows, appearing to be slightly out of scale to the main entrance, were probably added later in the building's life.

Another representative neo-classical house in Niagara-on-the-Lake is the MacDougal residence, named for its most important early occupant, Colonel Daniel MacDougal, a hero of the Battle of Lundy's Lane.

Intended as a town house, the severe parapet walls bookend an elegant three-bay brick façade, which is broken up into sections by elliptical double arcades. On narrow houses such as this, central hall plans were impractical, so the door was located to the side. In this case, it fits snugly into one of the arches. Four fluted pilasters dividing the standard six-panelled door from its sidelights support the fanlight. The glazing in the sidelights and transom is composed of almost painfully delicate and intricately linked geometric shapes. The twelve-over-twelve paned windows are

MacDougal House window detail.

longer in relation to their width than the early Georgian style windows. The graceful arcades and doorway lift and enliven the façade, saving it from an appearance of austerity.

At the other end of Lake Ontario, the neo-classic was becoming just as popular. Civic and business leader and the all-around main man in

Graceful arcades lighten the façade of MacDougal House.

The increased importance of the entrance is expressed here by the large doorcase and very refined porch.

Napanee at the time, Allan Macpherson grafted fine neo-classic detail to a standard Georgian form in his 1826 house. Macpherson's house, sitting between road and river, responded to both by having two façades, as the river was still an important transportation link. The design was made workable by a centre-through hall plan. The handsome doorways and the Venetian windows on the second floor are distinctive neo-classical features. Where expertise or funds to execute a proper semi-elliptical form were lacking, the transom window in the doorcase, as exemplified in the Macpherson house, was often a rectangle with delicate wooden muntins set at angles, to give the impression of a fanlight. Even so, the doorways, composed of gently fluted pilasters, rare double doors, and rather bold tracery in the sidelights, are very fine indeed. The doorways are flanked by plain pilasters supporting a narrow cornice suggesting porches may have been intended. Above the entrance are delicate flat-arched Venetian windows. Venetian or Palladian windows were introduced in the eighteenth century, based on designs by Palladio. They are defined as a wide central window, either flat or arched, flanked by two narrower, shorter sections with square tops.

Another neo-classic house incorporating Venetian windows was the very elegant Macaulay House in Picton. The Reverend William Macaulay was the son of United Empire Loyalists from the Prince Edward County area. After his first ministry at St. Peter's in Cobourg, in 1827 he was able to secure the Anglican parish located in the midst of his considerable landholdings at Picton, then called Hallowell. In 1839, he built a house that reflected his status as an important civic leader. Here he resided until his death. Macaulay wove the influences of three concurrent architectural styles into this stylish house. It is Georgian in its sense of symmetry and proportion. Its lightness and grace exemplify the neo-classic, as do its Venetian windows, the triglyph and metope cornice frieze inspired by ancient temples and the doorway with its intricate glazing of lozenges (ovals and diamonds). The cornice frieze is found on both neo-classic and Greek revival buildings. A triglyph is a three-grooved tablet repeated at regular intervals in a Doric frieze, the intervening spaces being filled with metopes, which could be plain or

decorated. In earliest times, the triglyph was the end of a support joist that was decorated, while the metope was the space formed between the supports. Eventually these elements evolved into a purely decorative form. The porch of the Macaulay House, with its paired thin columns, pedimented roof and overall feeling of delicacy is decidedly neo-classical.

For those with more modest budgets, simpler versions were created. The Whale Inn in Niagara-on-the-Lake is one such house. Following again the traditional Georgian form, the simple case door, lacking the characteristic fanlight, is composed of simple fluted pilasters, regularly glazed sidelights, and a shallow entablature. Such cost-efficient door designs, with or without the sidelights, became common throughout the province. The oval plaque over the door is a fire insurance marker

The Whale Inn, an unpretentious dwelling with quarter circles in the gable end which light the attic.

An integrated doorcase with or without sidelights and a door flanked by pilasters were common during the neo-classical period.

Governor John Simcoe gambled that there were many closet Loyalists still living in America and offered very cheap land prices to entice them to Upper Canada. Many of the first settlers believed these latecomers came mostly for the cheap land. Nonetheless, during the War of 1812 they proved their loyalty. Barnum's first house was accidentally destroyed by British soldiers who were billeted there during the war. Like most owners whose premises were damaged, Barnum received compensation for his losses and he rebuilt on the old "footprint" using the newly-stylish neo-classical.

The prosperous influential citizen built for himself an outstanding temple-plan house, rare in Ontario. The main two-storey section, flanked by single-storey wings, is positioned with the gable end toward the front, with an enclosed gable forming a pediment to mimic a temple. The triangle created within the enclosed gable is called the typanum. Within these spaces a semi-circular detail known as a lunette was often added. Sometimes it was glazed to allow light into the attic. The cornice and pediment are decorated with a rich and delicately worked frieze of repeating triglyphs and metopes.

As with most houses of the time, the emphasis was placed on the façade. Here, the smooth flushboard front gives way to clapboard on the other sides. One-and two-storey semi-elliptical arches, creating an arcade, run along the façade's centre and the wings organizing the bays. The front door is off-centre and is enriched by a pedimented door surround containing a blind semi-circular

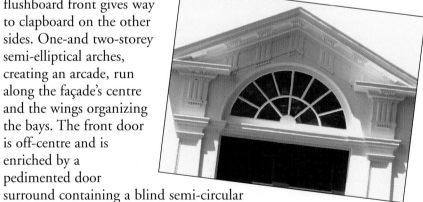

transom light. The fact that the ceiling height in Barnum's house precluded a functional transom did not affect the external composition

indicating the property was insured by a private fire company. This was an important feature, as firefighting companies would aid only their own clients. Other subtle features of the style include the cornice mouldings, end returns, and the quarter-circle, or quarter pie, windows in the gable ends to provide light to the attic.

One of the finest houses in Ontario, in Eliakim Barnum's house, "The Poplars," found west of Grafton, is a textbook example of the neo-classic. Barnum, a late Loyalist, arrived in Haldimand Township as a young man in 1807. The late Loyalists were those settlers who came to Canada in the thirty years of peace following the American Revolution.

of the door one bit. Its Roman Doric pilasters are miniatures of the pilasters forming the arcade. Barnum House is an extremely pleasing house, light and airy, and the play of light and shade and the delicate details provide a sense of visual rhythm that keeps the eye contentedly moving across the façade. Its decoration and use of Roman details make it neo-classical, though its temple form suggests Greek revival.

In 1940, Barnum House was acquired by the Architectural Conservancy of Ontario, a private organization founded in 1933 to preserve the province's architectural history, and it became the first restored house museum in Ontario.

Above: Barnum House, a fine example of the neo-classical style.
Opposite: Ceiling heights often prohibited fancy transom lights. However, architectural form required them. The result often was a blind, or imitation, transom as seen at Barnum House.
Right: Like the transom light, the fanlight, or lunette, is a fake too.

Greek Revival

1830-1860

Not so different from the neo-classical style of house is the Greek revival house. Some architectural historians consider them variations of the same style as the origins of their popularity both stemmed from the renewed interest during the eighteenth century in the ancient classical antiquities. The difference is that neo-classical is based largely on Roman examples, while the Greek revival took its inspiration as its name implies, from early Greece.

The popularity of the Greek revival was slow to develop compared to interest in Roman classicism. Initially, Europeans found the Greek architecture primitive in comparison to the Roman. For many centuries Greece had been out of bounds for the majority of Europeans, cut off from them by the Ottoman Empire's control of the Illyrian Peninsula. By the eighteenth century, the Turkish grip on the region was weakening, and wealthy Europeans started to visit Greece as part of the grand tour. Interested young men of means travelled to Greece to sketch the landmarks and ruins.

Much of the growth of interest in Greek antiquities can be laid at the foot of the Dilettanti Society — which has been described as a dinner club for the dissolute "grand tourist," the wealthy young Englishman expanding his educational horizons through travel abroad. Founded in 1734, the society was made up of many famous English grandees including the cuckolded Sir William Hamilton, husband of Admiral Nelson's famous mistress Lady Emma Hamilton. The only

Hamilton Place in Paris. A plain, bold, yet exquisitely handsome statement, in contrast to the refined and delicate neo-classical.

requisite for membership was to have set foot on classic ground. Yet out of their lubricated monthly meetings sprang some serious work on the study of the classical world, and by 1750 they had turned their attentions to Greece. Under their auspices, Englishmen James Stuart and Nicolas Revett went to Greece, where they made the first accurate measurements of Athenian ruins. Their influential work *Antiquities of Athens* (published in 1762) kick-started the Greek revival.

The primitive picturesqueness of Greek temples appealed to the Romantics, who first used copies of them, just as they had done with Gothic features in landscapes. Unlike the Gothic follies, these temples were exact miniature copies of the originals. As interest in these styles grew, more scholarly studies were undertaken. Authenticity over the picturesque became important. While the Gothic style was popular earlier than the Greek revival, the latter is the first recognized revival style, being the first to try to revive the authenticity of the style by basing designs on archaeological and historical precedents.

By the end of the century, the British had a fascination with all things Greek. Not surprisingly, the style made its way to the United States at this point. However, it wasn't until after the fall of Napoleon, when the struggle for Greek independence gripped Europe and caught the attention of Romantic poets like Shelley and Byron (who both died in Greece) that the Greek revival came into full swing. Greek culture was now seen as superior to the Roman, purer and more correct. This study and near worship of Greek classicism was viewed as a return to the cradle of Western thought, a return to its best ideals. It is not surprising that several Western countries associated these sentiments and Greece's struggle for independence with their own national aspirations. For a short time, this was true in England.

However, it was in the United States where this identification was the strongest and most long-lived. The new republic was still a fragile entity, America's fight for independence still relatively fresh in the public's mind particularly after their recent war with England, part of the War of 1812. Americans equated Greece's struggle for independence with their own. It was a natural evolution from the neo-classic to Greek revival. The porticoed public buildings at Washington, D.C., are only one physical manifestation of this perceived shared identity. The Greek craze coincided with the opening up for settlement of Upper New York State. Here the ideals of the oldest republic were to be transplanted into the wilderness of the newest. Frontier settlements bore such proud ancient names as Ithaca, Syracuse, Utica, and Troy. And the architectural style of choice was the severe, plainly decorated, temple-inspired Greek revival.

Willowbank, with its full colonnade, is one of the earliest and most expressive Greek revival houses built in Ontario.

As a result of all this study, many pattern books were published that not only outlined the Greek architectural orders, but contained practical tips on detail and finishing. The most significant in North America was Asher Benjamin's 1827 *The American Builder's Companion*, a book that contained enough detail on Greek architecture and building details to enable builders to construct handsome Greek revival structures without formal training. One of New England's most prominent architects, Benjamin deliberately called the book an *American* guide to underscore his belief that the Greek revival was particularly an American style. In it

Willowbank's, detail of Ionic capitals.

he modified English and Roman examples to make them distinctly American.

The Greek revival arrived in Upper Canada via both England and the United States. In many quarters of the colony, the Greek revival with its American and republican associations was looked upon with deep suspicion. Yet much of the Greek-revival influence in Ontario seeped up from south of the border particularly where there were strong commercial or geographic connections. Benjamin's book would have been readily available in Upper Canada by the 1830s. The style lent itself particularly to public buildings, but many notable houses exist. In most cases though, the Greek revival decoration was applied to earlier Georgian styles.

One of the earliest Greek revival houses remaining is Willowbank, in Queenston, built in 1834 for a prominent member of the embryonic colonial elite, Alexander Hamilton. Its architect probably owes much to Benjamin's guidebook. Hamilton's father founded Queenston, and his brother George founded Hamilton. The brothers strengthened their position in society by marrying daughters of the Honourable William Jarvis of Toronto, who served under Colonel John Graves Simcoe, Ontario's first lieutenant-governor. Willowbank, certainly, expressed Hamilton's place in the fledgling colony. Built high on a cliff overlooking the Niagara gorge, the style's connection to the picturesque is evident in its setting. Characteristics of the Greek revival include the house's monumental scale, cubic form, and low-hipped roof. The majestic two-storey porticoed colonnade with paired Ionic columns and plain entablature could have been taken directly from a Greek revival pattern book. To further accentuate its monumental scale, the house sits on a raised basement and the columns are supported by massive brick plinths. A processional stair leads up to the main entrance. Detail on the building is limited to the windows and doors of the east façade, which are massive. Typical of the Greek revival, the main entrance is recessed with generous sidelights, and a transom runs above not only the six-panelled door, but above the sidelights, which are separated by strong, broad elements. The whole composition is contained within a surround of pilasters supporting an entablature.

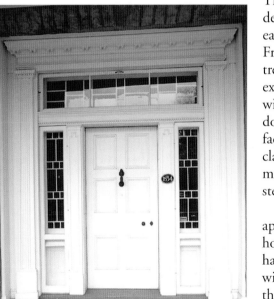

Willowbank's monumental entranceway, with generous sidelights and transom.

The doorway has much more depth or three-dimensionality than earlier styles. The east façade's French doors and windows are treated similarly. The rest of the exterior is much more restrained, with simple twelve-over-twelve double-hung windows. The west façade has a more traditional neo-classic feel, partially due to the more recent 1930s sweeping stone steps, plinth, and rebuilt porch.

Monumental details could be applied with success to smaller houses than this example. A handsome Greek revival house with very sophisticated detail, in the part of Cambridge which once was Preston, shares certain similarities with Willowbank, including the cube shape, shallow

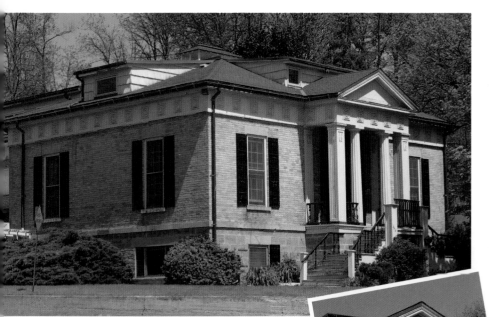

This portico was probably copied directly from one of the many pattern books available at the time. It commands the viewer's attention.

cast-iron acanthus leaves, a popular classical motif.

Few inhabitants of Ontario could have afforded such a bold and expensive expression of the Greek revival. Early in Ontario's history, there was a strong tendency to build in frame. This building preference was brought to Ontario by the Loyalists and late Loyalists, particularly those from New England. Brick houses would supplant framed ones only after successive waves of immigrants from the British Isles during the second quarter of the nineteenth century had settled and altered the character of the colony by choosing brick or stone. As settlements grew, many of the early frame buildings located in the centre of settlements gave way to grander brick houses or terraces. One victim was the modest Greek revival frame structure that served as a store, office, or dwelling. The temple form, which positions the gable end toward the street, lent itself to urban settings because it fit easily into narrow town lots. These were often decorated with a combination of neo-classic and Greek revival details. Occasionally, such as in the case of Barnum House, they had flanking wings.

Many of these buildings that did survive have suffered alterations and application of synthetic siding. A good example of an unaltered building exists in Cobourg. The house is positioned with its low-pitched gable end to the street in temple form, with the returning eaves suggesting a pediment. The six-over-six sash window, typical for the style, is undecorated and a

hipped roof, and a high basement. Indeed, it is quite possible that both houses had the same architect. A monumental portico supported by fluted Doric and panelled square columns has been applied to a Regency cottage form. Its buff brick is suggestive of stone. It shelters a typically configured recessed doorway. The wide roof frieze has a Greek design running along it, creating an impression of a metope and triglyph frieze, suggesting a temple. This decoration is also found on the square columns. The balustrades of the reconstructed entrance stair contain finely stylized

The Greek revival doorcase, scaled to fit a more modest house.

177 King Street in Cobourg. A frame house exemplifying the temple plan.

wool mill in the province. Mackechnie's Scottish roots may have influenced his choice of house style, as the Greek revival's popularity continued in Scotland long after it had declined in England. Mount Fortune was built on a monumental temple plan, bold and austere, with a unique moulded brick cornice and off-centre entranceway. Large panelled double doors, contained in a severe surround of plain wide pilasters and entablature, open to reveal a rare recessed vestibule containing the front door. Other typical elements are the lunette and

lunette is contained in the gable. The off-centre doorway, though scaled down, has a typical Greek revival composition, with plain flat pilasters and entablature. Atypically, wood quoins run up the corners of the house where, on most Greek houses, wide-panelled sideboards would exist.

An example of a grander temple plan also exists in Cobourg. Mount Fortune, built circa 1844 by Scotsman Stuart Mackechnie. He and his brothers, Henry and Andrew, immigrated to Cobourg and built what was then the largest

The temple-plan house, designed to mimic a Greek temple, with its gable end facing the street.

the long — almost to exaggeration — windows, which had a six-over-six double-hung sash. In the late 1850s, a north wing with Regency elements was added to the house.

In Cobourg's neighbouring town, Port Hope, a very dandy Greek revival terrace exists. Built on Port Hope's sloping main street for chemist T. W. Metcalfe, the skilled hand of the architect is evident in the handling of the potentially awkward site. There is no ungainliness here, only an elegant, uniform composition, with bold two-storey pilasters supporting an unadorned frieze painted

Moulded brick cornices at Mount Fortune, an unusual and expensive detail.

Metcalfe Terrace seamlessly responds to the slope of 134 Walton Street.

white to contrast with the deep Flemish bond brick. Inset into the cornice are a series of grilles: small windows that light the attic floor. The door surrounds have the "ear trim" or "shoulder trim" so characteristic of the style.

Ontario's Paris — named for the plaster beds that existed there, not the city of lights — was much influenced in its architecture by the Greek revival. Transplanted Americans from Upper New York State, particularly from the Rochester and Buffalo areas, brought the style and the distinctive cobblestone to the picturesque hamlet.

One of the best surviving examples of the Greek revival in Ontario may just be the diminutive cottage 16 Broadway near Paris's main street. Raised on its stone plinth-like basement, the one-storey-plus-attic gem is a cornucopia of Greek details, including stone pilasters supporting a broad eave cornice, severe stone window surrounds, a shallow-hipped roof, and cast-iron grilles. A belvedere, also known as a lantern or cupola, settles into the roof allowing light into the interior of the house. But the pièce de résistance here is the rugged Doric porch with its baseless stone columns, and a frieze of triglyphs and metopes, the latter decorated with garlands, geese, and girls. Decorated metopes were extremely rare in Ontario. Paris's characteristic cobblestone sheathing, combined with the severe grey stone, gives this robust cottage a rustic, almost primitive picturesque character in

Strong and broad with "ear trim," the door surround makes the entrance pop.

The strong Greek revival presence in Paris is likely a result of the town's ties to upper New York state.

keeping with the idealized Greek Doric.

A different treatment of the Greek revival is seen in another wonderful house in Paris, the 1844 Hamilton Place, probably Paris's most well-known residence. Here, a typical Regency cottage form is enveloped by its massive overhanging roof, supported by a broad unadorned frieze and a colonnade of panelled square columns surmounted by an oversized cupola. Its strong massive form, rigid symmetry, and plain trim suggest a Greek temple. The house, much larger than it appears, with a second storey tucked under the verandah roof, peeks out through the columns, revealing on its façade a monumental recessed doorway decorated with plain trim and Greek columns, flanked by two pairs of large double-hung six-over-six sash windows. The wood panelled columns resemble the corner boards found on frame Greek revival houses. Not surprisingly, the original owner, Norman Hamilton, a former citizen of Rochester, New York, employed Levi Brougham, Paris's master cobblestone builder, to sheath his house in this distinctive material.

Above: Hamilton Place, Paris.
Right: Cobblestone detail was an expensive and labour-intensive technique.

35

Regency Style

1815-1860

The Regency style arrived in Upper Canada shortly after 1815. It was part of the cultural baggage brought to the fledgling colony by decommissioned veterans of the Napoleonic Wars who, after the ousting of the eponymous French emperor at Waterloo, were offered land grants in the colonies in lieu of half their pensions. In the economic uncertainty following peace, these "half-pay" officers and other scions of the British middle classes immigrated to British colonies to boost their fortunes, maintain their social position or seek adventure. Yet all came with a determination to found a colony based on British ideals and institutions. At the same time, immigration from the former thirteen colonies had almost ceased as a result of the animosity created by the War of 1812. After the American Revolution, tens of thousands of "late loyalists," lured by the availability of cheap land, followed the vanquished United Empire Loyalists into Ontario. Now with nationalities firmly drawn, Americans looked westward to Ohio, while the 100,000 inhabitants in the province, bolstered by British patriotism over perceived victory in the War of 1812 turned towards the motherland for direction and heartily (at least initially) welcomed the new British settlers, who were arriving in ever-increasing numbers.

As a result, in the decades following the War of 1812 British influence in Ontario was at the highest it had ever been or would be.

Unlike the Loyalists, the British arrivals had not been expelled from

Eldon Hall, London. The location, low-set foundation, French doors, three-bay façade and hipped roof are often the only subtleties that differentiate the Regency from the Georgian.

their homes. They chose to come, and in coming they did not expect to adapt to the New World but to make it adapt to them. They were consciously nation builders, and their infusion of new political, intellectual, and cultural ideas changed the course and direction of the colony's development — extending, of course, to its architectural heritage.

In 1810, George III, suffering from porphyria, descended into his final bout of madness making it impossible for him to rule. His flamboyant and controversial heir, the Prince of Wales, later George IV, replaced him as head of state, in a period known as the Regency. Styled as the Prince Regent, the unpopular George was, however, the centre of fashion and taste, something a British monarch had not been for some time. In 1815, the Prince of Wales commissioned the brilliant architect John Nash to design an exotic Moorish summer house at Brighton. With this startling building, the mature Regency style was born. His patronage of Nash and his delight in the Regency style gave it an immediate cachet and legitimacy.

The roots of the Regency style are in the Romantic movement of the 1700s. Romanticism was a reaction against the order, harmony and rationalism of Georgian society. It affected literature, philosophy, religion and politics and had a profound effect on nineteenth-century thought. The Romantics valued emotion, variety, and individualism. Poets such as Keats, Byron, and Shelley gave expression to the movement, while the paintings of Salvador Rosa and Claude Lorrain were admired for their depictions of untamed nature and roused in their followers a sense of awe and the sublime.

Nature was a central tenet of the Romantic movement and revealed an interest in naturalized landscapes. The physical expression of the Romantic movement, landscapes and buildings, became known as the picturesque. In many ways it was a back-to-nature movement. The architecture of the picturesque from which the Regency style evolved began with garden structures, workers' cottages, and service buildings, which were designed to blend with and animate the naturalistic landscapes then being created by landscape architects such as the great Humphrey Repton. Outdoor views and vistas became important factors in situating a house, and soon the design of the house itself also became important. The

Dundurn Castle's garden face with its paired towers, rounded windows, and loggia are definitely Tuscan-inspired.

such as India. As the English became more familiar with these new colonies, their architectural decoration was fodder for the Romantic's taste. Egyptian, East Indian, and Moorish styles were all employed, but it was the native-born Gothic that became the most popular. In the Gothic, the Romantics found a highly decorative style that provided variety that stimulated emotion through its eerie associations with England's medieval past. The Romantics, too, appreciated the organic nature of medieval architecture and the way it related to the landscape.

Romantics wanted drama. Before, houses had been located for practical reasons, but now house sites were chosen to their ability to inspire. Ideally, the house became one with its landscape. Principal rooms, often located on the second floors in Georgian houses were located on the ground floor with French doors opening on to terraces and verandahs allowing direct access to the outdoors. Buildings were set lower to the ground, with a more horizontal emphasis; they featured less formal composition, and decoration that accentuated the play of shadow and light — the elements combining to produce the effect of pleasing irregularity and picturesqueness.

Many Romantics turned to more exotic styles to satisfy their desire for visual stimulation and variety. The end of the American Revolution forced Britain to create stronger ties with its other, more exotic, colonies

The peace with France after Napoleon was defeated in 1815 created, in England, a craze for all things French, which manifested itself in the Regency style. Yet the Regency was not a complete rejection of the Georgian and neo-classical traditions. That break would be left to nineteenth-century architectural movements.

Architects like Nash combined the aspects of the neo-classic, with elements from rural Italian or Tuscan architecture and the picturesque philosophy which at its heart was rural, to create a Regency picturesque style suitable for terrace housing and villas of urban centres. It was to the sophisticated building of the Regency that so many of these fashionable British immigrants to Upper Canada turned for inspiration when they built their colonial dwellings.

Many of the British immigrants who arrived in Upper Canada during the first half of the nineteenth century sought to identify

The most complete surviving example of a grand Regency house is Dundurn Castle in Hamilton, built in 1835 by the "boy hero" of the War of 1812, Allan Napier MacNab. A remarkable figure in the province's early history, MacNab distinguished himself in the military, as a lawyer, and a politician. A staunch Tory, he led the government troops with great energy and spirit during the Rebellions of 1837, crushing William Lyon Mackenzie's uprising and, as the Duke of Wellington stated, he was "the means for preserving the Canadas for the British Crown." For this he was knighted. He later went on to become the prime minister of the united Canadas in 1854 and was made a baronet, a hereditary knight, shortly thereafter. Back in 1840, as a move to strengthen British North America against the perceived American threat, Upper and Lower Canada were politically united as Canada East (Quebec) and Canada West (Ontario). MacNab considered himself a man of taste in the Regency sense, and a man of taste needed a house to reflect not only his growing social and political influence, but also his sense of style. Dundurn Castle was MacNab's answer.

Above: Changing tastes led to Dundurn's portico, an addition that gave a prominence to the entrance that was not originally intended.
Right: Roof finial.

themselves with the landed classes, whether they had a right to or not. The country house was a symbol of power and influence, and the new colonist sought to copy these houses in a more modest manner. Admirers of the Regency style built their houses on large tracts of land set in an appropriate landscape, regardless of the practicality. If no large acreage presented itself, villas or houses set into smaller parcels of land, were the next best thing. These villas often surrounded growing urban areas so, unfortunately, few have survived.

Much of the ethos of Regency architecture revolves around its relationship to the landscape. MacNab chose well for Dundurn's setting: the head of Lake Ontario overlooking Burlington Bay where fortifications were constructed during the War of 1812. MacNab's name for the house is doubly apropos, being the name of his family's Scottish ancestral seat and also the Gaelic word for the term "fort by the water." This elegant house sits comfortably in its landscape; in fact, it reaches out to it with its long horizontal three-dimensional composition, taking full advantage of the setting, providing magnificent views from all rooms of the house. In its overall composition it has subtly moved away from the strict Georgian convention of symmetry and emphasis on the main façade. Originally the main entrance was downplayed; however, a monumental Greek revival portico was added in the 1850s, giving the façade more prominence than was originally intended. French doors almost encircle the entire first floor, opening onto porches and terraces that further tie the house to its setting. Its tall chimneys and towers break the horizontal line of the house and add interest to its silhouette.

*Above: Colborne Lodge: picturesque
Regency at its best.
Right: Chimneys, an obvious necessity,
were also an important decorative feature.*

The house with its towers, stucco-over-brick sheathing, and rounded paired or triple windows is decidedly Tuscan. However, it is in the floor plan where the real break with Georgian convention occurs. Dundurn's plan is designed for function and to take advantage of views not just to fit within a prescribed form.

    In Toronto, Colborne Lodge is where the picturesque becomes the sublime. Architect John Howard built his house in what was then wilderness, on

the brow of a ravine overlooking a rugged landscape and the clear blue waters of Lake Ontario. No doubt the site was selected for its picturesque qualities rather than any practical reasons; the setting could have been taken straight from a Salvadore Rosa landscape. Named to honour the then lieutenant-governor of Upper Canada, Colborne Lodge's design has broken completely from the rigid formalism of Georgian architecture. The cottage form building is asymmetrical, with its unpretentious main entrance on the side. The focus of the house is the wide bay window and three generous French doors opening onto a verandah overlooking the lake. The low profile of the house, its stuccoed walls, deliberately rustic verandah, and triple chimney are an essay in the picturesque.

    Most people of the time could not build in the high style of MacNab or Howard. However, that didn't stop them from building in

Three-bay façades became common during the Regency period, replacing the more typical Georgian five-bay façade.

The verandah connected the house to its surroundings, making the garden more accessible.

the Regency taste, though often more simply and using more traditional forms. In London, John and Amelia Ryerse Harris settled down into a life of gentility at Eldon Hall. Built in 1834, it became the Harris family seat for over one hundred years. Its most famous chatelaine was Sophie, Mrs. Edmund Harris, the willful daughter of Egerton Ryerson. Perched at the edge of a ravine overlooking the Thames River, this symmetrical house sits low to the ground and is set sideways on its lot so that the main and garden (west) façades take full advantage of the site. The original cube form, simplicity, three-bay façade, hipped roof, and tall chimneys are typical Regency elements. The French doors and verandah, later alterations, only serve to enhance the house's original Regency spirit. An even later Victorian addition at the back, in a complementary style, gives the garden façade an irregular rambling appearance, which is rather pleasing.

The Boulton family were members of the notorious Family Compact, Ontario's early ruling elite. While conservative in their politics, they were certainly progressive in their architectural tastes, and built several splendid Regency villas, most of them, unfortunately, now demolished.

Edward Trevor Boulton, son of George Strange Boulton of Cobourg and nephew of Darcy, of the Grange (now part of the Art Gallery of Ontario), in Toronto, built a more modest villa in Cobourg, long known as Cosynook, on a portion of his father's extensive landholdings.

Built about 1855, the house is a typical Georgian symmetrical gable-end form yet with the large French doors, generous overhanging eaves and casement windows. The configuration of the half-pane-full pane glazing pattern of the French doors and casement windows is pure Regency. The neo-classical doorcase, with a flat-arched transom running over both the entrance and door, was by this time commonly used in conjunction with a number of different styles, including the Italianate and Gothic revival. The window treatment in the doorcase's transom and sidelights is a variation of the distinctly Regency glazing pattern. Edward's sister Georgina and her husband, the Reverend Walton Beck later occupied the house. Beck was also his wife's stepbrother, the son of George Boulton's widowed second wife. No doubt their nuptials raised a few eyebrows in conservative nineteenth-century Cobourg. In the 1870s the three gothic gables were added. Judge Jay Ketchum, a later inhabitant, gave the house its sentimental Victorian name.

The Regency style introduced the concept of picturesque asymmetry to architecture design, a major break from the disciplined symmetrical tradition of classical architecture that had been practiced for the previous several hundred years. This revolutionary concept would have a profound effect on the architecture of the nineteenth-century.

For those whose landholdings amounted to only a few acres or a town lot, the Regency still could be used to effect. The Regency cottage is the most identifiable Ontario house type that evolved out of the Regency. For the majority of middle-class families seeking their fortunes in Ontario, anything approaching a Regency manor was unrealistic. Yet such families desired a house that would immediately bespeak their status and sophistication in the world. This presented a quite a

gentleman's house. Enhanced by Regency decoration and proportions, the hipped-roof form was exported throughout the British Empire. Eminently suitable for the tropics, with its large French doors and overhanging verandahs, it was functionally less ideal for Ontario's more severe climate. However, this did not hinder its popularity in this part of the world, where it has become known as the Ontario Cottage or the Ontario Regency Cottage. So successful was it that it became one of the most common housing forms in the province.

The typical Regency cottage in Ontario during the 1830s was a one- or one-and-a-half storey structure with a low-hipped roof, symmetrical façade, tall chimneys, and a verandah, the latter often extending around the entire house, leading to the term "wrap-around" verandah. French

Above: Cosynook. During the Regency period, the entrance was once again downplayed in the overall composition. Inset: Regency casement window with later Gothic gable.

challenge. A challenge whose solution was found in India, where early British colonists adapted the Bengali dwelling, a one-storey temporary structure known as a bungalow (derived from a Hindi word), into a distinctive colonial

The quintessential Regency cottage. This one is located in Odessa.

doors were often preferred but not always necessary to the house's composition. Typical of the style is this charming example in Odessa, situated overlooking Mill Creek, probably built for a member of the Booth family, a prominent Loyalist family which ran the village for many years. This energetic bunch operated grist, saw and lumber mills, a lumbering business, wool mills, a cloth factory, and barley mills. They also acted as general merchants.

French doors exist on most of the façades and open onto a verandah, the roof of which is slightly curved, making the wide expanse of roof appear lighter and more graceful. This type of roof was often referred to as having a "bell curve," and was difficult to create. For a time it usurped in popularity the stalwart front porch. Its history is complicated, and it is believed that its origins lie in northern Portugal. It made its way to the Portuguese colonies in the days when that nation was a major maritime power. The evolving "outdoor gallery" moved through the Spanish and English colonies and arrived in England, where it was the height of fashion at the beginning of the nineteenth century. The verandah provided two important solutions in Regency design. It accentuated the horizontal line of the building and acted as a transitional space between two extremes, the indoors and out. The horizontality was further reinforced in most cottages by the decision to separate the roof of the house and the verandah. Because the verandahs were so delicate, they needed constant maintenance to survive, and many succumbed to the elements and time. Others were the victims of the modern need to have

The exaggerated eave on the Sutherland house, also found on other Regency cottages in the region, has led to the its nickname — the "house with a hat."

brightly lit natural interiors. The result is that such houses, without their verandahs, appear today unintentionally as being stark.

The supports for the verandah were simple, either rustic posts or simple turned columns. More picturesquely, they were made of treillage, supports made of simple wood strips fashioned together to create an elegant design often exhibiting oriental influences. Treillage created a moving pattern of light and shade along the house that animated its composition. In England, this Romantic detail was made out of cast iron, which not only created the desired effect, but also was strong and durable. In Ontario, where cast iron was still rare, colonists tried to recreate the effect in the less sturdy but more accessible alternative.

Usually the house was squarish, like the Odessa house. Although stucco was often the preferred cladding material in the Regency period, this cottage form lent itself to all materials, including clapboard, stone, and, of course, brick. In Cobourg, the Sutherlands, sticking to their Scottish roots, built a handsome, if somewhat severe, cut-stone Regency cottage. The large exaggerated roof overhang became a common feature of the style in Northumberland County and was aptly nicknamed "house with a hat." It is believed the deep overhang negated the need for a verandah. Plain paired brackets under the eaves carry the same sense of exaggeration as the roof. These simple Tuscan brackets evolved into the elaborately detailed brackets seen in later Italianate houses.

The severity of the house is enlivened by the later dormer, also a characteristic of the area and nicknamed "the nun's coif." When Regency

doors weren't used, the windows in Regency houses tended to be large in proportion to the rest of the house. New technology made glass more affordable and accessible, and larger windows served to connect the inside of the house with the outside. Above all, the Regency was an exercise in blending the house with its landscape. While the perfect setting for the Regency cottage may have been a picturesque landscape with awe-inspiring views, the compact form of the house lent itself to urban settings, as the Sutherland house illustrates. Here, the house retains the old-fashioned Georgian style paning.

While the Regency influence waned in the second half of the 1800s, the Regency cottage form remained relatively popular, perhaps because its simple form allowed the application of other stylistic decorations. This Dundas example has a plain, broad Greek revival doorcase, over which is a Gothic front gable. The entranceway is flanked by two remarkable windows containing paired ogee arched windows encased in a classically-inspired surround. The eclectic mix makes for a very appealing cottage. The stucco is likely a later addition hiding an original clapboard siding. In Stratford, tinsmith Thomas Birch built for himself a very up-to-date Ontario cottage employing all the latest decorative features, including the bi-chromatic brickwork in the simulated cornice under the eaves, known as diaperwork, and the yellow-brick quoins and

Top: A Dundas Ontario cottage with Greek and Gothic revival details.
Above: Weathered finial in a gable.

Above: A Dundas idiom — paired ogee-arched windows encased in a classical surround.
Right: A Stratford Regency Cottage showing later Victorian decoration.

window arches of the segmentally-arched Italianate windows and doorcase. Such examples show later centuries' taste for heavier, more ornate details, somewhat at odds with the intended simplicity of the concept of the Regency Ontario cottage.

The eight-sided structure has existed throughout the ages, examples being found in both ancient classical times and the Gothic medieval age. In the 1700s the style was of some interest to those who followed the neo-classic and Romantic tastes, to the former because of its geometrical and symmetrical form, and to the latter because of its intriguing shape. Because of its picturesque quality, octagonal structures began to appear in eighteenth-century landscapes as garden structures. Soon the shape was employed in houses, early Gothic and Regency homes among their number. Monticello, Thomas Jefferson's residence near Charlottesville, Virginia, and a masterpiece of neo-classical inspiration employed octagon and semi-octagonal shapes in various ways.

The connection to the picturesque probably led to the acceptance of the Octagon House in Ontario. While Americans often slot the form into the Italianate style, and others give it its own style, the history of its form links it strongly to the Regency. With the publication in 1849 of American Orson Fowler's *A Home For All*, the Octagon House was, briefly, the architectural rage. Fowler, himself, was more renowned as the greatest North American promoter of phrenology, the science of character divination through the shape of the skull. As the skull takes its

Early garden structures, such as Dundurn's, were the testing grounds for new revival styles. This octagonal temple was originally a cock-fighting pit.

shape from the brain, phrenologists believed, the skull's shape could give an accurate index of an individual's aptitudes and tendencies.

A Home For All was one of Fowler's many publications. In it he argued that the octagon, which was the closest to the perfect shape, the circle, was the best house form. Happy would be, he claimed, those who dwelled in this ideal house. On very practical grounds, he argued that the octagon plan provided more actual square footage than a square house of similar dimensions. Over 1,000 octagon houses were built in North America, some forty-five in Ontario, from the 1850s to the 1880s. Its shape lent itself to the application of different stylistic decoration, and examples with Italianate and Second Empire traits exist. In Port Hope, a town that boasts two octagonal houses (as does Picton), William Barrett's large octagonal house is one of the finest in the province. Nestled into the side of a hill so that the river-facing side stands two and a half storeys, the house is sheathed in stucco scored, or incised, to simulate stone, a common feature in Regency houses. A two-storey verandah wraps around the house, creating a very picturesque appearance enhanced by the octagonal belvedere that projects above the hipped roof. Originally the roof was flat, in keeping with Fowler's concept, but harsh Ontario winters no doubt led to a change. The French doors with typical Regency glazing are interestingly located at the building's corners, as are the lights in the attic storey. All in all, it is a very pleasing house,

The unique octagonal shape of the Barrett house in Port Hope fits nicely into its sloping site.

The angled French doors are testament to a skilled carpenter.

overlooking the Ganaraska River and the historic town of Port Hope.

One of the most picturesque house forms to emerge from the Regency was the Tuscan, or Italian, villa, inspired by the rustic farmhouses that dotted the romantic landscapes of such artists as Salvador Rosa. John Nash's Cronkhill, built in 1802, became the prototype for this idealized Italian farmhouse popular in England and North America. This asymmetrical house, whose most dramatic element is its tower, arose from the newly-developing early-nineteenth-century English suburbs. A villa is generally defined as a detached house, often with outbuildings, picturesquely situated on relatively small, informally landscaped grounds. The burgeoning urban middle classes of England in the late 1700s and early 1800s, inspired by romantic spirit and a growing bank account yearned for the picturesque settings of their country counterparts, the gentry. These newly rich were not restrained by family history and were more than happy to publicly demonstrate their newfound wealth. Fashionable architects of the day, such as Nash, were more than happy to supply them with what they wanted. During the eclectic Regency period there were Gothic and neo-classical villas, but the most popular villa form was based on the rustic Italian or Tuscan country houses of the sixteenth century.

The Regency "Tuscan villa" was imported to Canada about 1830. Like its cousin, the more demure Regency cottage, the Tuscan villa form became so popular here it continued for another fifty years after the Regency style's popularity waned. One of the earliest examples in Kingston, is Bellevue, or Tea Caddy Castle, built circa 1838, once the home of Canada's first prime minister, Sir John A. Macdonald. This picturesque villa embodies all the elements of the Tuscan while providing an essay on Regency details. The dominating element is the tower that rises from the juncture of the two wings, forming a characteristic L-shaped asymmetrical plan. The entrance to the house is through the tower which is an ornamental descendant of the medieval Italian watchtower, built for a very practical reason: defence. Originally, the tower would have been open and would have

Regency Style

housed a bell to warn of imminent attack by marauders.

In Bellevue is found a full expression of the Regency picturesque. Its heavy simple form nestles into its landscape. French doors and a casement window pierce the solid stucco-clad walls, which are sheltered by large overhanging eaves that on the Tuscan original performed a very practical purpose — shading the interiors from the hot sun. Stucco, favoured for its rustic and primitive feel, was the preferred sheathing of the Regency period. Ironically, the use of stucco only became viable due to late-eighteenth-century technological developments that strengthened the material, making it more durable. Stucco was often incised to imitate stone. Casement windows, also a distinctive Regency element, sacrificed practicality for fashion in Ontario's blustery wintry climate. The windowpanes are distinctly Regency with their half-pane, full-pane, full-pane, and half-pane glazing pattern.

Picturesque Bellevue was a dramatic addition to Kingston when it was built.

The pierced scalloped edge that finishes the large, overhanging, awning-style roof and the hooded balcony roof with the same scalloping edge, give the house an almost oriental look. It's simple pattern creates a lively play of light and shadow on the rough-cast walls. This house also has an early two-storey bay window. The whole composition has a merry, whimsical quality that must have been very much appreciated in its time as it is today. Similar plans to Bellevue appeared in various architectural pattern books, including J. C. Louden's *Encyclopaedia of Cottage, Farm and Villa Architecture and Furniture* (1833) and the more influential *Country Residences* (1840) by Andrew Jackson Downing, and

Tower detail.

Tower rooms offer panoramic views.

A Juliette balcony.

Oriental influences are evident at Bellevue.

Architecture of Country Residences (1850).

As the century progressed, the simple Tuscan gave way to the more ornate and heavier Italianate elements. Brick replaced stucco, the houses became proportionally taller, and the tower stretched ever further upwards. St. Mark's Rectory at Niagara-on-the-Lake, built in 1858, is a typical yet relatively plainer version of the mid-century villa. Its emphasis on the vertical — the stately asymmetrical tower, tall chimneys and elongated windows, pedimented gable — direct the eye upwards, while the horizontal lines — in the raised brick banding, window sills, and lintels and cornice — are de-emphasized and treated simply. Even the doorway is downplayed, although the later porch tends to distract from the vertical movement. Embellishment on this Anglican rectory is reserved for the paired semi-circular windows and the Juliette balconies with their round-headed French doors at the top of the tower, the place

The gable's fretwork is mirrored in the ground floor window heads.

Above: Mulholland House, Cobourg, is an exuberant Italianate villa, though lacking the signature brackets. Inset: A splendid Renaissance revival doorcase.

the eye eventually comes to rest. St. Mark's Rectory may have resulted from a sense of Anglican decorum, but in a time when church revenues were notoriously lacking, limited funds could as easily have been the cause.

Funds were certainly not an issue in the construction, almost twenty years later, of Cobourg merchant Robert Mulholland's house in 1877. Built from profits made from western land speculation, this bold, if not brazen, example of the Tuscan villa stands out in an architecturally conservative town. Exuberance is the key descriptive. The vertical movement upwards is challenged by the many strong horizontal elements, including the stone foundation, jagged band courses at window-lintel height, the white eave cornices, the first-floor bay window, and the magnificently robust doorway. A richly carved pedimented door surround, reminiscent of Italian Renaissance, with deeply panelled paired doors and etched glass sidelights cannot fail to impress those who would enter. The typical Tuscan tower is commanding but lacks the verticality and the balconies of earlier towers. The gable is decorated with very fine fretwork, while the idiosyncratic stone window heads have a vaguely art nouveau feel, although they predate that style by a good ten years.

49

Gothic Revival

1830-1890

The term Gothic or "Gothick" began as one of derision applied to medieval architecture by classicists of the Renaissance who considered the Goths, an early Northern European tribe who overran most of Southern Europe between the third and fifth centuries, to be barbarians. The classicists laid the blame for the Dark Ages squarely at the doorstep of this Teutonic people — whom they also blamed for destroying the great ancient classical traditions. The Goth culture, which served as a general term for all medieval culture, was considered valueless and primitive to these adherents of Greek and Roman culture. They particularly deplored medieval architecture because it failed to follow classical rules and proportions.

Despite its discredited reputation, Gothic architecture refused to die out, particularly in Northern Europe where craftsmen, needed to repair cathedrals, were still trained in medieval construction. This continuing thread of Gothic knowledge came to be known as "Gothic survival."

By the seventeenth century a small group of intellectuals and academics took up the Gothic culture as a scholarly exercise, and it wasn't until the mid-eighteenth century that English Romantics, frantic in their quest for interesting and picturesque decoration, discovered the expressive nature and asymmetry of Gothic architecture, and soon whimsical cottages and garden structures designed in the Gothic style enhanced informal picturesque landscapes. The Romantics were not concerned with academic or scholarly work but with composition and

A vibrant and lively Carpenter's Gothic cottage, Erland Lee House sits on the brow of Stoney Creek Mountain.

effect that heightened sensibilities, stimulated the imagination, and led to the "cultivation of feelings." It was not long before the Gothic made the leap to more substantial houses. Batty Langley published one of the first major pattern books on Gothic architecture in 1740. However, his work did not re-create the plans and elevations, but rather the decorative elements — Gothic doors, windows, mantelpieces, and trim that could be applied as decorative features to buildings. Langley's inspirations came largely from the last phase of Gothic revival, the perpendicular Gothic often associated with the Tudors. Horace Walpole's 1754 Strawberry Hill was the first major house to be built completely in the picturesque Gothic and generally marks the beginning of the Gothic revival in England. Walpole, a keen Romantic and Gothic scholar, was the son of Sir Robert Walpole, the great British prime minister. Walpole the younger also invented a literary genre, the Gothic novel, with his wildly popular *The Castle of Otranto* in 1764. Novels such as *Otranto* or Mary Shelley's *Frankenstein*, with their overwrought plots often set in old castles or ruins, fuelled the interest in the Gothic. Not surprisingly, picturesque houses often mimicked castles with crenellations and mock fortifications.

This early period of the Gothic revival had really more affinity with the Regency style, for it used the decorative forms of the Gothic to fulfill the Romantic movement's ideal of architecture expressed through the picturesque. In the same way, architects of the period, such as Nash, used the Tuscan, high classical, and the more exotic Moorish and Egyptian architecture to similar effect. In many cases the expressive Gothic decoration was applied to Georgian forms, so that they could be integrated into carefully created, naturalistic landscapes for the desired picturesque composition.

Following in this tradition, in 1833 landscape gardener James C. Louden published his *Encyclopedia of Cottage, Farm and Villa Architecture*. Although not the first of its kind, it became one of the most significant and widely read pattern books of the nineteenth century offering prospective builders plans, elevations, and practical advice on building both rural and suburban houses. His designs, influenced by the picturesque, included some asymmetrical plans, and were offered in a number of different styles, including Greek and Swiss. But Louden recommended the styles closer to his time and geography as being more appropriate, emphasizing the Gothic, particularly Tudor (Perpendicular) Gothic, following the early Gothic revival tastes. His pleasing plans in that style catered especially to the middle classes.

Pinehurst is one of the earliest picturesque Gothic houses surviving in Ontario.

Louden had a particularly powerful impact in North America. In the United States, Andrew Jackson Downing, relying heavily on Louden's works and theories, published several similar works, including *Cottage Residences* in 1842 and *The Architecture of Country Houses* in 1850, which popularized Gothic architecture in the United States. Both Louden's and Downing's philosophies centred on the belief that living simply in the country and being connected to nature enhanced the soul. Downing added a democratic twist to Louden's practicality, by joining republican values with a useful and well-functioning domestic architecture that did not try to copy the trappings of foreign elites. Louden's and Downing's work, and others less popular, were widely read in Ontario. No domestic source for architectural patterns existed in the province until thirty years later.

Picturesque, or Regency, first made its appearance in Ontario around 1830 and was commonly seen by the 1840s in public buildings, churches, and houses. As in England, the most popular early Gothic revival style in Ontario was the Perpendicular.

Port Hope's hilly terrain provided many a perfect setting for lawyer Nesbitt Kirchhoffer's Pinehurst, an early Regency Gothic house set on a hill amid a grove of pine trees. Not surprisingly, newly arrived British immigrants brought along their romantic enthusiasm for the castles and fortifications. Quite a number of castle-like buildings were built in Ontario, the most ambitious house among them being what is today the Whitby's Ladies Academy. Yet this influence is evident in Kirchhoffer's handsome two-storey brick house. The details are what make Pinehurst a Gothic house, as its form, proportions, and symmetrically arranged façade are Georgian. However, the roof is steeper and the eaves are tight to the walls. A large brick parapet inscribed with the building's construction date of 1846 rises above the front entrance and is flanked on either side by smaller parapet gables, all finished with stone coping. The paired cross-casement windows, arched Tudor-style front door, and slender paired windows are all Gothic details. The brick front entrance with its wood corner supports that rise into the finials of the balustrade above is an unusual feature. But the house with its solid massing, angled buttresses, finialed porch, and set on a rise of land with a low-walled terrace suggesting battlements, allude to a fortified citadel. One almost expects to see decorative crenellation just to finish off the fortification motif.

Auchmar, Hamilton. A substantial dwelling that has been deliberately designed to look like a low, rambling Elizabethan house.

The central parapet, inscribed with Pinehurst's date.

Isaac Buchanan built his Regency Gothic manor, Auchmar, on Hamilton Mountain where he could watch the progress of the city whose fortunes were so tied to his own. A Scottish immigrant, Buchanan was one of Canada's early nation builders. A man of immense vision and energy, his involvement in finance, railways, and politics helped lay the foundations of the future nation.

His eighty-six-acre estate, named after his father's Scottish home, the sale of which financed his success in Ontario, was less pretentious than that of his fellow Scot and Hamiltonian Sir Alan MacNab's Tuscan-styled Dundurn. The long, low, one-and-a-half-storey, U-shaped Gothic stucco house has a tall, steeply pitched bracketed roof with projecting gable wings that flank a central core containing a series of smaller gables. The gables have simple decorative fretwork. The end gables now lack the robust finials that once pierced their roofline, though six tall multiple-flued chimneys, together with the gables, still create an interesting and animated silhouette. The two central chimneys are quite

interesting, each being made up of a cluster of four flues set on an angle to the roof. The Gothic is further reinforced by bays with Tudor-arched windows, pointed windows in the gables, hood moulds, and a Juliet balcony, added later, and supported by brackets at the centre gable. The bay windows and balcony are crenellated, adding just a bit of castle motif to Auchmar's picturesque cottage form. Despite its picturesque Gothic detail and the introduction of asymmetrical elements such as the off-centre front door and the differing end wings, the form and balance of the house remains persistently Georgian.

Buchanan's hesitation in using asymmetry did not, interestingly, extend to his outbuildings. Auchmar's gatehouse survives, separated from its manor by rows of crisp suburban housing, the result of successive subdivisions to the estate. Such outbuildings, though practical, were also landscape features and, as such, could be far more unconventional without raising the eyebrows of the conservative elite. The design with its asymmetrical T-plan, steeply pitched roof, and angled chimney, presents a decidedly picturesque appearance. Its details,

Top left: Multiple gables and chimneys create an animated roofline.
Far left: Simple gothic detailed front door.
Left: Ogee-arched bay windows.
Right: Auchmar's surviving gatehouse.

Gothic villas were once very popular.

Large, wooden bay windows allow immediate access to the garden.

such as the pointed lancet-like gable windows, hood mouldings, and stucco finish, are similar to that of the main house. The design of this picturesque little building could easily have been pulled from Louden or Downing, and while its plan was still considered quite avant-garde in Ontario, it portended the direction of house plans that would become common in only a decade.

However, only a decade later, Westover, the 1867 estate of the Hutton family, had become representative of the solid, stylish, picturesque Gothic villas that were so popular in Ontario during the third quarter of the nineteenth century. Still set on its original nineteen

acres overlooking the Thames River in St. Marys, the asymmetrical ashlar stone house has multiple gables with sawn gingerbread (more correctly called bargeboard or vergeboard), with finials at gabled peaks, bay windows, a Tudor-arched second-floor window, and decorative cast iron. The front door of the two-and-a-half-storey house is sheltered by a chunky porch supported by two square columns. Built in the year of Canada's confederation, Westover's Gothic revival with its English associations was the new Dominion's unofficial national style.

A distinctly American version of the picturesque Gothic, the Carpenter's Gothic developed out of the strong tradition of building in

The Patterson house, north of Toronto, is an outstanding and unusually substantial surviving Carpenter's Gothic farmhouse.

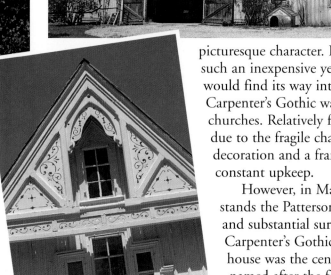

Top Right: A handsome structure in board and batten.
Inset: Wooden fretwork on Patterson House.

wood that had existed in the United States since the first settlements. Immense forests provided Americans with an inexpensive building material. New technological developments in the nineteenth century including band-and-scroll saws, allowed steam-powered sawmills to produce finely cut architectural details and sheathing, which in turn allowed carpenters — hence the style's name — to easily and affordably build houses lavished with wooden decoration. The fact that many of the details were meant to be stone did not hinder them in any way. In fact, the Carpenter's Gothic was limited only by the imagination of the carpenter, resulting in many idiosyncratic and eccentric houses. The models for many Carpenter's Gothic houses came straight from pattern books like Downing's. Indeed, Downing favoured wooden structures, particularly those sheathed in board and batten, which intensified a building's rustic and

picturesque character. It was only natural that such an inexpensive yet expressive form would find its way into Ontario. The Carpenter's Gothic was also used for small churches. Relatively few examples survive due to the fragile character of the style's decoration and a frame structure's need for constant upkeep.

However, in Maple, north of Toronto stands the Patterson House, an exuberant and substantial surviving example of Carpenter's Gothic. At one time the house was the centre of a thriving village named after the family, who owned a farm-implements factory, and owned much of the surrounding countryside. They built this house in the early 1850s. At that time, the family fully expected the railway would be built near their property, ensuring them even greater prosperity in the future; however, the railway was routed elsewhere. Though the Pattersons continued to prosper, the village of Patterson eventually passed into history. The house stands as an expression of the optimism for a community's unfulfilled future. The large two-and-a-half-storey Downing-inspired house, with steeply pitched one-and-a-half-storey gables, is set in a rural landscape that Downing would have approved. The board-and-batten siding enhances the structure's rustic quality, producing a stronger surface pattern of light and shade while emphasizing the house's verticality. The house has an abundance of decorative wood trim, found in the trusswork in the gable, the fancy detail in the verandah, the hood mouldings and lacy muntins in the sidelights and transom. The pierced bargeboards in the gable were added at the turn of the century.

The original colour schemes as dictated by Downing for such buildings were natural or neutral tones that integrated the structure into the surrounding natural landscape. Many were painted white at the turn

Highly decorated late Victorian Gothic with polychromatic brickwork.

of the century when that colour once again became fashionable. The white-lead paint so popular with the Greek revival was acceptable in the Gothic when the house was enveloped in a mass of foliage, producing what was considered a magical impression. Certainly that is the case here, with the Patterson house set like a pavilion in its landscape.

In England, a more serious and scholarly approach to the Gothic style developed in the early nineteenth century affected Ontario architecture later in the century. Academics and antiquarians increasingly played a role in fashioning Gothic taste. The interest in Gothic was part of a broader cultural movement connected to literature, scholarship, and collecting. Scholars were distressed at what they saw as the cavalier manner in which the style was so freely used. Several academic works were published during this time. One of the most influential was by Thomas Rickman, a Quaker whose *An Attempt to Discriminate the Styles of English Architecture from the Conquest to the Reformation*, published in 1817, quickly became a textbook for the style. Rickman created the Gothic style terminology we use today — Early English (1170–1280), Decorated (1290–1350), and Perpendicular (1340–1540). It gave the style a chronological history and added greatly to the growing body of knowledge on the subject. This period of the Gothic revival is generally referred to as the archaeological phase, in which a more literal approach to Gothic design was taken, based on

An elegant bell-curved verandah with simple treillage.

more accurate information provided by archaeological discoveries. The public had become increasingly curious about the history of medieval England. The Gothic novels of Walpole gave way to the more historically accurate and equally popular early nineteenth-century novels of Sir Walter Scott. Scott depicted everyday life in medieval England in his chivalrous high adventure series Waverley, which included such works as *Ivanhoe*. These captivated the public for over a century. From garden features to houses to churches and educational institutions, the style's influence evolved until it

Decorated window head reflects the influence of Italian or Venetian Gothic.

permeated the English consciousness. Such was its rise to prominence that, in 1835, after a disastrous fire destroyed Westminster Palace, the English Houses of Parliament, the Gothic revival was deemed the only appropriate style in which to rebuild Britain's seat of power, arguably the most symbolically important building in the country. The style recognized the medieval origins of England's unique parliamentary system and the Gothic became, for a time, the national style of England. Not surprisingly, Canada would adopt the Gothic Revival style for its own Parliament buildings in Ottawa (1859–66), as an expression of the young Dominion's nationalistic aspirations it shared with its mother country.

One of the men responsible for the interiors of the new British Houses of Parliament was Augustus Pugin, a giant of the Gothic revival movement, architect, writer, and philosopher. To the intellectual and archaeological Gothic revival, Pugin infused a moral and religious fervor.

His publications, including *Contrasts* (1836) and *True Principles of Pointed Architecture* (1841), had an enormous impact on society. A convert to Roman Catholicism, Pugin believed that Gothic architecture, particularly from the Decorated (also called Pointed) period, was the only true Christian form of architecture. Its beauty was derived from the religious faith of its builders. The Decorated style, as its name implies, was highly ornamented and decorative, one of its defining features was the lancet, or pointed window. He firmly believed the medieval period was the high point in human achievement and by recreating its art and culture, the moral and religious values of that time could be revived. In Pugin's words, the Gothic is "not a style but a principle." Architecture then could be judged, good or bad. Pagan Classical Greek architecture, for example, was bad, Christian architecture good. Pugin also championed the use of naturalistic forms as decorative elements, and was one of the first to articulate the idea that a building's design should reflect its function, through its structure and plan. Ornamentation, therefore, should stem from structural function. He was also the first to promote "propriety" in architecture — the idea that some styles or forms or decorations are inappropriate for some building uses.

John Ruskin, the most important Victorian art critic, railed against Victorian taste and design, in which he believed material concerns overrode spiritual ones; Ruskin expanded on Pugin's ideas. He also promoted European Gothic, particularly the patterned and polychromatic Venetian Gothic, as providing worthy architectural models. His influential publication *The Seven Lamps of Architecture* (1849) outlined his seven principles of architecture, while his three volume *The Stones of Venice* (1851–1853) applied his seven "lamps" to Venetian Gothic. This led to the development of a very rich, textural Gothic style that employed the use of contrasting coloured stone and brick decorative features.

After Pugin's death in 1850, the Gothic style moved away from rigid archaeological principles, and a freer, interpretive style developed that is now called High Victorian Gothic. Later, more severe forms of earlier Gothic were incorporated into the revival, causing the term Muscular Gothic to be coined.

In Ontario, the High Victorian Gothic found full expression in churches, educational institutions, public buildings, and some architect-designed houses. In 1881, John Thom, a lawyer and tax officer at Osgoode Hall, built a splendidly individualistic High Victorian Gothic

Above: This Late Victorian Gothic in London combines many Italianate features.

house in Toronto's newly developing suburb of Rosedale. The use of contrasting red and buff brick is one of the defining features of the High Victorian Gothic style and is directly related to Ruskin's interest in Venetian Gothic. Here it is used for very dramatic effect with the quoins, segmentally arched window heads, band courses, and front door decoration in rich, red brick in contrast to the buff brick walls. Polychromatic brickwork is generally the term used to describe this decorative treatment, although purists would call this example bi-chromatic, as only two colours of brick are used. The striking second-floor arched window with a wide surround band of polychromatic brickwork and the blind, pointed arch in the side bay window similarly treated are vaguely Venetian in feel. The pointed arched door contains glazed double doors and a transom with tracery and stained glass. The Gothic revival's origins in religious architecture were evident in the door. The use of stained glass in houses was increasingly popular as the influence of Pugin and Ruskin became more widespread (Ruskin didn't design buildings). The lancet windows in the cupola, heavier bargeboards pierced with quatrefoils, and coloured slate roof are further evidence of the more mature Gothic revival. The whole composition is further festively embellished with shingled gables, wrought-iron cresting, and a side porch — the rich woodwork must have been a real eye-popper in conservative Toronto.

This 1885 London house illustrates how the High Victorian Gothic elements were more typically used in Ontario houses. The asymmetrical form of the Robert Lamours house with its paired brackets could easily pass as an Italianate or even Queen Anne. However, the major elements in the design — the strong use of polychromatic brickwork in the window arches and band courses and the complicated gable, almost a

A late Victorian Gothic gable in all its glorious complexity.

Above: Gilknockie in Guelph: a formidable Gothic revival villa. Inset: Gothic sash windows.

gable within a gable, above the two-storey bay windows — are Gothic. This combination of bay and gable became very common, particularly with semi-detached and terrace houses in Toronto, so much so it has since been termed the bay-and-gable style. Lamours, the Assistant Superintendent of the Grand Trunk Railway, rented the house from industrialist and London alderman Samuel Crawford, who subdivided the back portion of his property to build two houses.

Wholesale grocer James B. Massie's Gilknockie home, built circa 1875, represents the more austere stream of late Gothic revival architecture. The typical asymmetrical villa plan, with bay windows, a wooden oriel window (a projecting second-floor bay window), and a three-storey square tower containing the main entrance, is executed completely in smooth ashlar stone, with little excess ornamentation. The front verandah was added later and may have replaced a more decorated one, but the pierced bargeboards, entrance hood mould, and iron cresting on the steeply pitched hipped tower roof are the only nods to fanciful decoration. The lancet window in the gable and the sash design of the bay windows are further Gothic features. Whether the use of stone was designed to give the building a Muscular Gothic feel is not known, but the recessed front door was a feature of that style. However, Gilknockie is a severely handsome, masculine house that would have appealed to a piously protestant Scotsman of this era.

It is in the more modest middle-class houses located largely in the countryside and small towns of rural Ontario that the influence of the Gothic revival style is truly seen. Promoted in pattern books and in the *Canadian Farmer* as the most suitable style for rural residences, for both practical and philosophical reasons, the Gothic revival farmhouse has become almost an icon in Ontario's architectural vocabulary. These houses followed the plans and forms set out in early pattern books and with few exceptions varied little from then right up to 1900.

The L-shape or T-shape plan provided a commodious house. It could be frame, stone or brick and was generally a one-and-a-half-storey building with a large front gable. Decoration varied considerably depending on time and place.

Gables and dormers, decorated vergeboards or gingerbread, finials, bay windows, verandahs or porches, quoins, decorated window and door surrounds, and windows of various shapes were the most common elements. The brickwork ranged from plain buff or red brick to riotous polychromatic designs.

Gilknockie's entrance.

The elaborate wood ornamentation and detail on the verandah shows the growing popularity of Eastlake decoration. Taste arbitrator Charles Eastlake wrote *Hinton on Household Tastes* in 1868 as a reaction against the excesses of Victorian taste. He was largely concerned with interiors and furniture. However, much to his chagrin, his name was identified with a style of architectural decoration that was opposite his sensibilities: relief carvings, mouldings, geometric ornaments, scrollwork, beaded spindles, and turned-and-chamfered posts all characterize Eastlake. Eastlake decoration became extremely popular in Ontario and was incorporated into Italiante, Second Empire, Gothic and Queen Anne styles.

Above: A typical Ontario farmhouse, as found in small towns and rural areas all over the province.
Inset: Verandah fretwork detail.

Typical is this cheerful-looking red brick house on the outskirts of Beamsville. Here, the windows are segmentally arched, the corners given prominence with raised brick quoins, and the verandah decorated in turned woodwork. The second-floor door is one of those oddities that are not that uncommon, and probably exists because the owner decided he'd prefer a sloped verandah over a flat-roofed porch with balcony; he may have decided this during construction but didn't feel the need to change the door.

Farther along the same road, a farmhouse at Grimsby has some interesting elements that depart from the norm, among them the Flemish bond brickwork and

Flemish bond brickwork and projecting window hoods in Grimsby.

projecting window hoods supported by turned wooden brackets. Considering the house faces east, it would seem these are purely decorative. In the smaller front gable is the ubiquitous pointed window. The pointed window was often a more economical way to replicate the lancet window.

By far the most common form of Gothic revival house was what has become known as the Ontario vernacular cottage. It was more modest and affordable, and therefore more common.

It is a one-and-a-half storey gable-end cottage, symmetrically balanced with a central door flanked by a window on either side, similar to the small Georgian house with the exception of a tall, pointed gable over the front door. The standardized plan was highly affordable, yet could be individualized through the a host of available details and finishes.

The Brand house, west of Port Hope, is the quintessential Ontario vernacular cottage. Built circa 1860 by farmer John Brand, the attractiveness of this deceptively large house is a result of its elegant portions and light decorative flourishes. A lancet window with graceful Gothic muntins, the hallmark of the Gothic Revival, ornaments the front gable. These windows are more common to central and eastern Ontario houses than to those in the southwest. The original verandah, with its low-pitched bell-curved roof is, like many Victorian verandahs and porches, supported by chamfered columns — square posts whose corners have been cut off at forty-five degree angles. Chamfered columns were often decorated with elaborate bases and heads, but in this case they are slender and simply treated.

A rare survivor on Gothic revival houses is the wood and glazed storm porch. Many Victorians enclosed the front door with a temporary storm porch as protection against the cold winds and snow. Usually they were removed during the summer months, but this more refined

If Ontario had an official house style, a Gothic cottage like this house would be it.

example became a permanent fixture.

Edgemount, with its superb view overlooking Stoney Creek and Lake Ontario from atop the Niagara escarpment, is a festive Carpenter's Gothic version of the Ontario Vernacular House, festooned with flamboyant ornamental woodwork. For over 160 years the Lee family, United Empire Loyalists, farmed the two-hundred acre farm. The original 1808 log house was enlarged and remodelled into its present form in 1873. The house is sheathed in the characteristic board and batten siding, with wooden boards laid vertically with thin strips called battens placed over their joints, Two bay windows flank the main entrance, which is protected by an open porch with slender octagonal columns. The bays and porch are made into one architectural statement by the lacy wood filigree cornice that forms a continuous band stretching across the top of the bay windows and flat-roofed porch. The porch is also decorated with a bold, geometric-patterned grill. The front double door is unusually wide with a plain Greek revival door surround. It has two sets of glazed doors, the outer set, no doubt, acted as storm doors, giving some extra protection to the house on its exposed site on Stoney Creek Mountain. The windows in the gables are very idiosyncratic, being horizontally divided in two by a band of decorated wood. The fretwork, or bargeboard, is decorated in a patriotic maple leaf motif while the roof is shingled in wood: the most common form of roof in nineteenth-century Ontario.

Erland and Janet Lee, the third generation of Lees to occupy the house, gained fame for being among the key founders of the Women's Institute, now a worldwide organization dedicated to women's education and development. The organization, which was founded in 1897, was recently made famous in the movie *Calendar Girls*. The Institute's first constitution was drafted in the Lee's house and Mrs. Lee wrote out the first version in longhand at her dining room table.

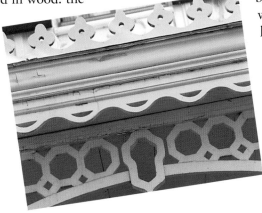

The front porch's fancy fretwork.

The local limestone quarries of St. Mary's have been the economic backbone of this charming town for much of its history. Many of the most attractive houses are, not surprisingly, built of the local limestone quarried along the banks of the Thames River. James Mackay, one of town's seventeen early hoteliers, built this sturdy limestone Ontario vernacular cottage in 1865. The house's wooden features are boldly treated as if to match the strength of the limestone. The front porch, added about twenty years after the fact, is very handsome with tapered, panelled, square columns; large, overhanging, bracketed eaves; and balcony railings. A nice touch is the open arch with drip spools, terminating in elegant consoles between the columns. The steeply pitched gable, with sculptured bargeboard in exaggerated S-shaped curves, culminates with a finial which instead of soaring towards the heavens, flows downward, forming a beautifully carved teardrop pendant.

A surfeit of wood decoration at the Erland Lee House.

The Gothic revival died hard in Ontario, particularly in the rural areas where it continued to be used, though with decreasing frequency until 1890s. The Gothic revival has been called the most important artistic movement to come out of England. Gothic revival tenets such as the organic approach to design and the "honest" use of materials, influenced the development of modern architectural movements and led to both the Queen Anne Style and the Arts and Crafts movement.

Italianate Style

1860-1890

Vying with the Gothic revival for popularity in the mid-nineteenth century was the highly decorated and lively Italianate. Based on the architecture of the Tuscan country villas of the rich Florentine elite of the Renaissance, the Victorian Italianate evolved from the picturesque Regency's earlier interest in Tuscan architecture and from the desire to continue a classical tradition. In England, a significant group of thinkers felt a secular form of architecture was necessary to counterbalance the Gothic. The Greek revival lacked flexibility, and interest in porticoes and high classical models waned in mid-century England. This group looked not just to the rural Italian architecture of the Renaissance but also to that era's urban palazzos.

Ironically, in England, it was architect Charles Barry, with the 1834 Gothic Houses of Parliament which immediately identified Gothic with England's national ideals, who popularized the Italianate. Barry's true interest lay in the Italianate and his designs for the Travellers' Club (1829–32) and Reform Club (1837–41) were based on sixteenth-century Italian astylar (meaning column-free) town houses in England. A plain façade was enlivened by the pedimented windows' surrounds, quoins, and decorated cornices. Queen Victoria and Prince Albert's Osborne House, in Italian villa style, also forwarded the style. The high-style version of the Italianate became known as the Renaissance revival, and in Ontario it was almost entirely reserved for commercial and public buildings. However, its more modest country cousin, the

Castle Kilbride in Waterloo.

Italianate, spread quickly and became a popular style choice for domestic architecture beginning in the 1860s, largely due, once again, to American Andrew Jackson Downing and his influential books, such as *The Architecture of Country Houses*, published in 1850. It made the style widely available not only in the United States but also in Ontario. The style was also very flexible and could be adapted to all kinds of designs and houses, from the modest to the very large. The style used or reworked elements of its Tuscan architecture rather than copying period buildings exactly, and so was not considered a revival. There were no major style identifiers, such as the mansard roof or the portico, nor were there any rigid proportions that had to be followed. Thus, it allowed designers leeway and creativity. It lent itself to being highly decorated, coinciding with a growing affluent society's desire for ornamentation. Its elements were taken and integrated with other styles, particularly the Gothic, Second Empire, and Queen Anne. By the 1860s, in the United States, it had overtaken the Gothic as the most popular house style. Ontario was fertile ground for the Italianate, as it was stylistically related to the earlier Regency. But the Gothic remained the favourite, especially in the rural areas.

The Italianate was a style of elements, the most defining of which was the highly decorated paired eave brackets which evolved from the simple brackets of early Tuscan villas commonly used during the Regency. As a result, the Italianate was often called the "bracketed style." Other elements of the Italianate include tall, narrow segmentally arched windows, paired windows, moulded window surrounds, or heads, quoins, wide overhanging eaves, and cupolas or belvederes.

One of the most common Italianate forms was the simple square hipped-roof house. It was generally rectangular with the narrow side fronting the street. The façade was usually symmetrical, except for the front door, placed to one side and forming a side hall plan similar to that of the Greek revival. These houses were ideal for town and city lots and could range in size and ostentation, depending on the size of the owner's purse. Often they were topped by a belvedere (literally meaning "a good view") or cupola.

This Brockville house is a restrained example of the style. Constructed of buff brick, which became very fashionable in the 1870s, it has a three-bay façade with paired front doors off to one side. The window's lintels rise gently in a segmentally arched pattern (or, as some say, a raised eyebrow form) popularized by the Italianate. A back side wing, atypically generous here, was a common feature. Its classically inspired porch, however, is a turn-of-the-century replacement. The windows are undecorated, the delicate brackets unimposing, and the belvedere small, yet its very simplicity and sense of proportion are what make it such an elegant, dignified-looking house. Its

formidable cantilevered Arts-and-Crafts front porch is also a later addition.

While the Brockville house is restrained, its more modest

An understated Italianate house enlivened by a later Arts and Crafts front porch and an Edwardian side verandah.

counterpart in London leaves no post unturned or surface undecorated in its attempt to impress. In the United States, most Italianate houses, particularly the smaller ones, were of wood. In Ontario, the penchant for brick was so strong that wood houses were less popular and those not covered in artificial siding now even more rare. Here, the cladding is laid smooth, with a siding commonly used on frame Italianate houses known as flush board, which provided a perfect foil for highly decorative surface elements such as the ones

Window head and cornice detail, London.

found on this spirited example. Paired and single, flat and segmentally arched windows with decorated window surrounds, a deep eave cornice with paired brackets, and an intricate wooden bay window animate the front façade. The real attention-getter, however, is the entrance porch, with its perforated cornice of quatrefoils and wood-turned decoration supported by slender Corinthian columns and pilasters, all sheltering a very wide double door with generous transom. Wrought-iron cresting on the bay and porch add further eye appeal.

A more substantial example of the simple hipped-roof Italianate is the 1882 Hamilton house designed by architect James Balfour for a prosperous druggist. Balfour, a well-known Hamilton architect, designed

Elaborately decorated details on a relatively simple form are an Italianate characteristic.

Above: Single brackets support a panelled cornice.
Left: A stylish Italianate town house in Hamilton.
Right: Detail of stone quoins and a sawtooth banding course.

the first Detroit Museum of Art. In this house, constructed in the fashionable south end of Hamilton, the form takes on real pretension. Taller and grander in scale, the house is outfitted in expensive materials and details, including the fine stone quoins, window heads with keystones, and sills. The round-arched windows are long and narrow with one-over-one double-hung sash windows and the doorcase is segmentally arched with moulded doors containing glass panels. The partially glazed transom retains its Victorian gold street numbers. A generous hipped roof with highly detailed brackets and cornice contains a central dormer and tall moulded chimneys. So close is the Italianate to the Second Empire style that had this house's roof been a mansard instead of being hipped, it would have been called a Second Empire house.

The traditional Georgian form lingered on in Ontario and regained some ground during the Italianate's popularity. Symmetrical three- and five-bay houses with hipped roofs and paired brackets began to appear as early as the mid 1850s. In 1865, the *Canada Farmer Journal* published plans for a square Italianate house probably derived from these earlier models. Compared to many of the popular house plans of the time it was rather simple and plain. Yet its sturdy character hit a chord with many no-nonsense Ontarians who may have been weary of the whimsies of more romantic styles, particularly the Gothic, and wanted an alternative.

The Doctor's House at Ancaster, built in the 1860s, was influenced by the *Farmer's Journal* and is certainly representative of a house form that remained popular over the next generation. A symmetrical two-storey hipped-roof house with a central, projecting frontispiece terminating in a broken pediment, the house harkens to familiar Georgian traditions. However, the intricately turned and paired brackets are Italianate. It has a particularly handsome centre window, above a large doorcase with full sidelights and generous transom. The small side wing that disrupts the overall symmetry was originally the doctor's office and surgery. Other later details are more highly decorated with ornate window heads and surrounds, complex eave

Above: Early Italianate home, heavily influenced by the Georgian style.
Right: Paired brackets — the Italianate trademark.

cornices with chunky pair brackets, and intricately turned porches.

Not all Italianate forms had a projecting centre or frontispiece. Castle Kilbride, built in 1877 for James Livingston, the "linseed oil king of Canada," near Waterloo is such an example. A Scottish immigrant of modest means, enterprising spirit and hard work, Livingston created a fortune that allowed him to build this highly embellished robust Italianate house just two decades after arriving in Ontario. A tall ornate belvedere

Above: Castle Kilbride belevedere detail.
Right: Castle Kilbride's vivid colour scheme stands out among its more sedate contemporaries.

dominates the house that sits high on its foundations and dominates the landscape. Two bay windows flank the main entrance. The double front door is restrained, however it is made more grand by the highly ornate porch and processional steps. Above the entrance is a pair of round-headed windows with decorated head flanked on either side by two similarly treated windows. The bracketed cornice and quoins at the corners complete the composition. Yet it is the interior of his house where Livingston outdid himself, commissioning some of the finest *trompe l'oeil* walls and ceilings surviving in Canada today.

Italianate houses for the most part never achieved the sophisticated or high style that one associates with other styles. They were comfortable, often ramblingly generous houses, with bay windows poking out here and there. Italianates were very responsive to the

A classic, comfortable Italianate home in Napanee.

Front porch laden with decorative trim.

Detail of Castle Kilbride's trompe l'oeil interior paintwork.

domestic lives of those who occupied them. Such was the secret to their success. In Napanee, a commodiously handsome example in rich warm brick is immediately welcoming. Its big two-storey bay windows, long windows and bracketed cornice are all trademarks of the Italianate. The front porch is unusual for its double design, and also because it has survived at all. Many Italianate and Gothic houses, particularly those whose design came from pattern books, were meant to have verandahs and porches, but these features were unaffordable to the owners. Yet the balcony door was built anyway, perhaps with the hope that one day funds would become available. These stranded second-floor doors became known as "suicide doors" and can be seen in architecture all over the province.

In western Ontario, the brick of choice was buff coloured, sometimes referred to as cream or white. Brick colour often depended on the colour of the local clay. In central and eastern Ontario, the clay tends to be reddish, while in western Ontario clay deposits are predominately white or buff. However, during the 1860s, buff brick became fashionable, as it gave the appearance of stone walls. How fortunate for the residents of western Ontario that one of its most rapid periods of economic development not only occurred when its native clay was most fashionable, but coincided with the popularity of the Italianate. Comfortable, old buff-brick Italianate houses line the streets of towns and cities in western Ontario, more so than in eastern Ontario. Many were L-shaped, with big wings extending at the back, like this Stratford example, which has a two-storey bay, segmentally arched windows, bracketed cornice, and narrow,

Top: A cozy Stratford Italianate house.

Above: A highly sculpted porch and verandah.

one-over-one sash windows. A neat feature here is the highly decorated storm porch. Because of the province's harsh winters, many houses of this period included a permanent storm porch that was treated as part of the overall design. Richly embellished like this one, the storm porch became the focal point for the house. The porch decoration and complicated turnings on the verandah illustrate how ornate the decoration on houses was becoming by the 1870s.

The Bean-Wright House in Waterloo is a more restrained and yet formidable example. It towers over the street rather than settling into its landscape. But the elements are typical, except that the projecting portion is terminated by a pedimented gable with two small round-

The impressive Bean-Wright House, Waterloo.

headed windows reminiscent of a tower. Ghosting on the brickwork reveals this handsome charmer has lost its original verandah, which may have once softened its severe look considerably.

Many buildings in Ontario confound stylistic interpretation. Subjectivity plays a part, so it can be difficult even for the most seasoned expert. In Cambridge, this bright and lively façade is animated by features that could fit comfortably in the Gothic, Queen Anne, and Italianate. But it is the wonderfully over-decorated Italianate window heads and sills that grab the eye. They are detailed in such a way that one might think that they are pressed metal, a cheaper nineteenth-century substitute for wood and stone commonly used in commercial buildings. While the house is designed to fit on smaller town-lots, its bold decoration enhances the streetscape.

Above Left: A Gothic-inspired gable.
Above: Window head detail.
Far Right: An attractive and eclectic Italianate house.
Inset: Ornate decorative trim.

Second Empire

1865-1880

Baby boomers, nurtured on Hollywood horror and the B movies of the 1950s and '60s, can be forgiven for feelings of anxiety and apprehension aroused by encounters with an imposing, classic, Second-Empire-style house. So foreign in streamlined, modern, postwar North America, examples of this rich, ornate, and often formidable style provided atmospheric settings for some of celluloid's most sinister characters, from Norman Bates and his mother in *Psycho*, to the lighter "mysterious and kooky" *Addams Family*. In more sympathetic roles, it was either hopelessly backward, as in *Giant* or quaintly derelict, as in *It's a Wonderful Life*. Nonetheless, in its day, it was considered the height of modernity and sophistication.

After the fall of Napoleon I, France suffered from years of political division and economic uncertainty under the restored Bourbon monarchy. By the mid 1800s the nostalgic French yearned for the days of past Napoleonic glory. Louis Napoleon, the first French Emperor's opportunistic nephew, rode to power on the coattails of his uncle and established the Second Empire in France in 1852, styling himself Napoleon III, in deference to Napoleon I's son and namesake who should have been Napoleon II. With his fascinating and beautiful wife, the Empress Eugenie he created a glittering court, the envy of Europe. The Second Empire architectural style was born out of the optimistic and heady early years of Napoleon III's reign, when, buoyed by public support and the resulting economic prosperity, the new Emperor rebuilt Paris in a grand and opulent manner reflecting his national and dynastic

A formal French-inspired Second Empire house in Kingston.

ambitions. The Second Empire borrowed heavily from French historical precedents, from the French renaissance to the more recent, glorified first French empire. The additions to the Louvre in 1856 represent one of the earliest examples of the new style. Its most distinctive feature was the mansard roof, a two-sloped hipped roof based on a sixteenth-century prototype. The feature had already been revived once in France in the late 1600s by French architect Francois Mansard, who used the architectural device frequently enough that it came to bear his name. The steep pitch of the second slope allowed for a full upper storey of usable attic space. With Napoleon's seal of approval, the Second Empire style quickly became the most popular, and official, architectural style in France.

From France the design's elements were soon exported to England, where it became a short-lived architectural craze. The intriguing emperor and his dazzling wife enthralled not only the general population but also England's greatest couple, the dowdy Queen Victoria and her serious husband, Prince Albert. The close yet unlikely friendship that almost immediately arose between the two couples no doubt only further served to popularize French fashion in England.

From England, the Second Empire quickly jumped the pond and became immediately popular in the United States. This style was seen not as a revival architecture, like the Greek or Gothic, but as a form springing out of current political and aesthetic movements, very modern and avant-garde. Its opulent style perfectly expressed the post-Civil War taste; the nouveau riche wanted to show off. For the two decades following the Civil War, the Second Empire was the most

This Hamilton Second Empire home combines the Italianate and vestiges of the Gothic in a more typically Ontario version of the style.

favoured style in the United States. It lent itself to both non-residential and residential forms. In fact, so many public buildings were built in the Second Empire style during the presidency of Ulysses S. Grant that it was sometimes referred to as the President Grant Style.

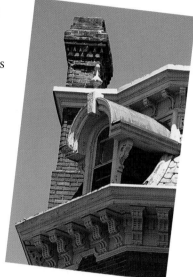

It was largely via the United States that the Second Empire arrived in Canada, and some contemporary accounts described it as an American style. In Canada it had its greatest impact during the 1870s but never achieved the same popularity as in the United States. In house design, it played second fiddle to the more established and popular Gothic and Italianate styles. In fact, while most public buildings in the United States and Canada were more purely French inspired, Second Empire houses often borrowed heavily from the Italianate, and occasionally from the Gothic, to produce a more North American and less pure version of the style.

Above: Large decorated roof and eave cornices.
Right: A potpourri of skillfully turned woodwork.

This can be seen in the rather grand semi-detached houses in Hamilton. Originally a balanced terrace of three houses, the third unit was unceremoniously chopped off to provide room for an apartment tower. What's left is a somewhat lopsided double house containing what was the middle, symmetrical five-bay unit with projecting frontispiece and one end unit — an asymmetrical villa. The effect is an improbable pair of non-identical twins. However, it is a handsome structure and the whole is tied together by the dominant feature of the house: the mansard roof with slate tiles and highly decorated eave and roof-ridge

cornices. This rather squat version of the mansard appears to be a local variation of the form, as several other such roofs in Hamilton are similarly lacking the height usually associated with it. The mansard could have five different roof slopes: straight, straight with flare, convex, concave, or S-curved. Often two or more roof slopes appear on one house. From most perspectives, this Hamilton mansard has a convex or bell-curved silhouette, while the projecting frontispiece's roof is straight.

Dormer windows were stylistically *de rigueur* in the Second Empire house, not to mention a practical necessity so that the interior of these tall attics had some natural lighting. They came in a variety of shapes and were often richly embellished with ornamental trim as is the case in the Herkimer Street house with its single round-headed dormers and elaborately decorated hoods and surrounds. Strong brackets under the eaves, stone quoins, elaborately decorated bay window, and porches are equally at home on Italianate or Second Empire houses, as are the single and paired, segmentally arched, one-over-one sash windows with dripstone hood mouldings and rusticated keystones. The porch decoration even sports Gothic-inspired trefoils. The warm red brick and

This stately Kingston mansion shows the hand of a skillful architect.

supported by rusticated pilasters. Two bow windows trimmed in smooth and rusticated stone flank the doorway, while smooth stone pilasters supporting plain stone lintels flank the paired and single windows on the second storey. All roofs retain their original iron cresting.

In the last twenty years there has been a tremendous growth in interest in heritage houses. It has spawned a restoration industry and a legion of experts who not only restore houses but replicate and enlarge existing ones in period styles. This Second Empire Guelph house is an example where recent owners have enlarged the house using correct Second Empire details. In its present form it is somewhat reminiscent of the houses built for American robber barons and railway kings during the early years of the gilded age in the 1870s. While most of the house is original, the front tower has been raised, extending above the roofline, and the front porches which extend out into the grounds to form a porte-cochère and a verandah, respectively, are also new. Yet except for the clues in the third floor of the tower and the over-scaled column supports, very few people could tell where the old ends and the new begins. The main body of the house is a relatively plain symmetrical square. The surprisingly sophisticated stone porch is original and contains an attractive round-headed double door with etched glass panels and carved keystone. The second-floor balcony carved out of the tower is an oddity and is original. Four square columns support the tower, which is made of wood on the third floor, has paired windows with decorated hoods and windowsills, and rises to a large mansard with circular windows and iron cresting, all of which are recent. It

Finely crafted, panelled and glazed, round-headed paired doors, Guelph.

lively rhythmic façade make it less intimidating and more inviting than many of its type.

In the skillful hands of knowledgeable architects, stylish houses more in keeping with French precedents, such as this elegant stone townhouse found in Kingston, were possible. The whole composition is decidedly formal and symmetrical. Rich classical details embellish the façade, on either side of which exist elaborately decorated flat-roofed porches typical of the style. A mansard roof with patterned slate and single and pedimented paired dormers surmount the two-storey structure. The formidable front door is uncharacteristically prominent, with a carved stone door surround with a keystone sheltered by a round pediment

Second Empire

replaced a smaller mansard roof that went only to the third floor. Flat-roofed porches, supported by columns, extend along the façade from the tower and out into the grounds. While slightly exaggerated, it is this type of porch that could have once existed on this house. To the rear of the house is an original secondary tower common in Second Empire houses, with an octagonal roof that rises above the main house's roofline, forming a crown. All the roofs are decorated with colourful patterned slate tiles. The whole animated composition, commanding a fine view overlooking Guelph, is a flamboyant and individualistic essay in the Second Empire and would certainly rate high on the

Far left: A recently restored and enlarged Second Empire house. Inset: Authentic period details on the rebuilt tower roof.

Above: Second Empire semi-detached houses in Guelph.
Inset: Detail of a square bay window.
Far Right: An earlier cottage updated with a circa 1870 mansard.

Hollywood "spooky" meter come Halloween.

Though especially popular among the well-to-do, the Second Empire style was equally adaptable to all housing forms, and for all classes. Developers especially liked the fact that they could gain a full storey in the attic without being taxed for the extra floor. Buildings at the

time were taxed by the number of floors; attic space was not classed as a floor. Semi-detached and small terraces in the style sprung up in the larger urban areas of the province. These semi-detached houses in Guelph are an example of modest Second-Empire housing. Economics has reduced the usually sculptured mansard roof to a straight, steep-pitched element of the façade. However, here the builder has jazzed up the façade with affordable decoration, including pedimented dormer windows, iron cresting, a colourful patterned slate roof, and buff brick window and door surrounds.

The mansard roof's practicality and affordability allowed owners to update their older dwelling in the latest fashion. In some cases, the result could be somewhat bizarre. This was not the case, however, with Avon Castle in Stratford. Businessman William Easson updated his

modest Regency cottage to create this imposing charmer. The dormer windows in this particular example are especially fine, with decorated window hoods supported by carved consoles.

The "Second Empire" description was sometimes applied to asymmetrical forms more in keeping with the Italianate or the

The tall, triple-flue chimney flanked by semi-circular pedimented dormers.

earlier Regency styles. This house in St. Marys is illustrative of this tendency. It is surprising how many houses in Ontario appear to have been built as wedding presents. This house is one of them, built by one of St. Marys' leading citizens, George Carter, as a wedding present for his daughter, Charlotte, and her husband, Henry Rice. The brick villa contains all the trademarks of the Second Empire, the mansard roof, and flat-roofed porches. The tower with mansard roof rises significantly above the rest of the house and retains its original iron cresting. The Carter House was built in 1881 when the Second Empire style had

almost run its course. The style ranks almost as an architectural fad that lasted not much more than a few decades. Its costly detail became dated very quickly and its fall from favour was swift and unforgiving, like that of the dynasty that gave it its name. Today it is once again appreciated.

Left: Dormer window detail.
Below: A picturesque Second Empire villa.

The Romanesque Revival

1880-1900

As the Victorians' appetite for new experiences and ways of expression grew, they looked further and further into the past for inspiration and models. As ancient classical and Gothic periods had been exhausted, interest grew about that murky period of European history known as the Dark Ages, specifically its later years just prior to the Gothic era and its Romanesque architecture.

Romanesque architecture dates to the eleventh and twelfth centuries but its roots began in the ninth-century reign of the greatest of medieval kings, Charlemagne. This Teutonic king took the first steps of bringing western Europe, war-torn for centuries, out of the Dark Ages by uniting it under a strong central authority and Christian faith. He sought to re-establish Latin Christianity based in Rome and long subjugated by Byzantium. Charlemagne's rule created years of peace and prosperity, during which arts and culture flourished.

Architectural expression in Western Europe since the fall of Imperial Rome had stagnated. It was only during the Carolingian era, as the time of Charlemagne's reign was called, that it began to blossom again. With the focus on establishing the Holy Roman Empire, there was a conscious attempt to design in the Roman style, hence the term Romanesque. However, the Carolingians didn't look to the Imperial Roman orders but rather to simpler buildings. Of particular interest to them was the Roman arch. It took several hundred years of evolution until the Romanesque style was fully developed and not until the

Massive stone and masonry construction, towers, deeply recessed openings, decorated surfaces and animated rooflines are all elements of the Romanesque.

eleventh and twelve century did it find full expression. In reality, the style was influenced not only by Roman, but also by early Christian and Byzantine architecture. By the time it reached its peak, the style had spread throughout western Europe, and local forms had evolved in different areas. General characteristics of the style included the rounded arch, massive plain masonry structures, arcades, grouped columns, short pilasters, shallow buttresses, and the vaulted dome.

Perhaps because of Charlemagne's German background, the revival of the Romanesque developed first in Germany, about 1830, where it was known as the Rundbogenstil, or round arch style. It quickly spread to England and the United States. In England, the Romanesque was also known as the Norman style, being brought to the island by William the Conqueror in 1066, and its revival was often referred to as the Norman revival. As was Greek to Roman architecture, the Romanesque was seen first as primitive and crude compared to the Gothic which followed it. However, as with the Greek style, intellectuals came to see a purity in the Romanesque. Victorians became interested in the castellated fortifications, churches, and great monasteries that dotted the European landscape and brought civilization and education to the west. In its early stages, the Romanesque revival was primarily used in religious and public buildings.

In North America, one of the earliest buildings carried out in the Romanesque manner was the Smithsonian building in Washington, D.C., begun in 1841. In Ontario, an early example was University College in Toronto, begun in 1856. Romanesque revival, representing links with the past and the continuity of history, was highly suitable for a museum and an institution of learning.

Celtic designs, grotesques and human faces decorate the stone surfaces of George Gooderham's house in Toronto.

Recessed, rounded arch entrance. *Richly decorated surfaces.*

It would be almost twenty years later, though, before the Romanesque revival was used for residential buildings. The noted American architect Henry Hobson Richardson was largely responsible for this change of affairs. He developed a free and strongly personal interpretation of French and Spanish Romanesque design which became known as Richardson Romanesque. His few houses inspired a whole generation of architects throughout North America. The major identifying feature of Richardson Romanesque is the coloured rusticated cut-stone masonry used for foundations and building trim. Other features of the style include massive stone or masonry walls, the round-arched, dramatic, semi-circular, recessed door openings, bands of windows, short robust columns, and towers.

It's not surprising that the Romanesque became popular during the Gilded Age of the American nouveau riche. Impressive and expensive castle-like Romanesque structures represented wealth, power, and stability to an insecure new elite. Because of its massive masonry and stone construction, it required plenty of labour and skilled craftsmen, which restricted its use to the upper classes and to areas, usually urban, where such workman could be found. An extremely rich robber baron, ensconced in his Romanesque castle, could be reasonably secure that his workers weren't enjoying themselves in cheap knock-offs of the style, security that neither the Queen Anne nor the Second Empire could provide.

When Ontario's richest man, George Gooderham, decided to build a new house in the late 1880s in Toronto's up, and coming, Annex district — so named because that land was annexed to the city in 1887 — he chose the latest and most impressive Victorian style: the Romanesque revival. Gooderham took the family distilling business and created a commercial and industrial empire, expanding the operations into the largest facility of its kind in the British Empire and diversifying into railways, banking, and insurance. Like most Victorian industrialists, he supported many philanthropic initiatives. The Romanesque arrived in Toronto with construction of Toronto's City Hall and the Ontario Legislature Buildings, both begun in 1886.

Gooderham's splendid residence at the fashionable intersection of Bloor and St. George streets was a statement announcing the family's growing economic and social prominence. Fronting onto St. George Street, his richly textured masonry house with stone trim sits on a solid rusticated stone base. The sprawling asymmetrical plan includes a large circular corner tower facing the intersection anchoring the building to its corner site while providing a connection and smooth transition between the two principal facades. A variety of roof shapes, gables, tall chimneys, and the tower all animate the building and create its castle-like profile. The Romanesque's main identifier, the round arch, is used extensively, either singly, in pairs, or as a triple arch, defining many of the windows and doors. The rusticated stone arches are supported by sturdy short columns or piers characteristic of the style. Rusticated stone is used throughout as trim for arches, quoins of grotesques and human heads, banding courses, windowsills, and lintels. Intricate carvings based on early Christian and Celtic designs decorate the gables, column heads, and eaves. Much of the focus of the decoration is concentrated on the main entrance contained in a large three-storey section that terminates in a large gable flanked by the corner tower and a stone porte cochère. The deeply, almost cavernously, recessed front door is accessed through one of a pair of lavishly decorated arches.

The Hendrie House, with its massive masonry walls and rusticated stone trim.

Gooderham called his house Waveny, after the river in Norfolk near his birthplace. It was quite common for houses to be named after the owner's ancestral home or area. In this way, tradition, continuity, and often social status conferred by an old respected name were fostered and maintained.

Carved and textured stone create visual interest in this Hamilton house.

These stone-faced round arches originally opened to a recessed porch.

Above: A simplified Romanesque house in Kingston.
Right: Domed corner tower detail.

A somewhat less ostentatious version of the style is the Hendrie House in Hamilton. Here, the size of lot and the finances of the owner limited the architect, W. A. Edwards, though he managed to squeeze a substantial masonry townhouse, with an animated composition of square and round towers, roof shapes, chimneys, and gables, into a small corner lot to almost riotous effect. Its round-arched entrance (obscured by the recent addition of an awning) opens directly to the corner from a square tower. The entrance arch is part of a triple arch supported by short columns with moulded heads and decorative brick under the sills. Besides the entranceway, the triple arch has two south-facing windows. These windows might once have been an open porch. The window arches are dressed stone with raised drip moulds and decorative ballflowers where the drip moulds meet. The surface lacks the rich textured decoration of Waveny, but rusticated band courses, sills, and lintels intermix with smooth stone trim and stained and leaded glass that add extra panache.

Corner lots seemed to be popular sites for Romanesque houses. This corner lot site in Kingston displays a much more modest and simplified version of the

style. A traditional, largely symmetrical masonry square house with hipped roof is given the Romanesque treatment, with a recessed round-arched entrance and rusticated stone-trim banding courses, sills, and lintels. To give this corner house more presence and reinforce its Romanesque character, the architect or builder had suggested a tower by rounding

For economic reasons, Romanesque houses tended to use less complicated forms. This example, however, exploits its corner lot with a curved wall and tower.

Although symmetrical, Romanesque drama is achieved through decorative features and finishes.

the corner of the house at the intersection and adding an oddly slender turret with an onion-shaped dome popping from the roof above it.

By the late 1800s, building on speculation was a common practice all over the province. In London, shortly before the turn of the century, a pair of semi-detached Romanesque houses were built on spec on one of that city's most fashionable streets. With profits in mind, the architect of these houses followed the traditional format for semis, namely the

Patterns of rock-faced stone enhance this parapet.

Recessed doorways and upper arch combine to create an imposing entrance.

asymmetrical façade with mirror-image plans. Here, however, the details are robustly Romanesque, with the first-floor façade sheathed in rusticated stone that contrast with the red brick second floor. The omnipresent stone-trimmed arch is found on the second floor above the entrances, sheltering recessed balconies. The roof contains several gables and brick finials. The deeply recessed front doors are sheltered not by an arched entranceway but by a central stone pier and pilasters styled to resemble primitive supports. Taken as a whole, the design is quite successful.

In Toronto, many houses were built on speculation. Even though most Ontarians preferred the homeyness of the Queen Anne style, they admired certain aspects of the Romanesque. In the fashionable Annex where Gooderham lived, many houses combined Romanesque and Queen Anne elements very successfully so that the former lent strength and solidity to the blend but was softened by the latter's whimsy. On Toronto's Madison Avenue there are many fine examples, including this one,

balanced by a two-storey bay on the façade creates a cozy feeling. Interesting elements include the balcony's triple arches supported by brick columns and the wide entrance arch that doesn't quite form a complete arch.

Romanesque's popularity lasted less than two decades. It arrived late and was swept out of fashion by the growing reaction against the heavy, ostentatious Victorian styles and the desire to return to a simpler, less decorative, style of housing.

Above: A rare small-town example of a Romanesque with Queen Anne touches, Stratford.

Top Left: The Queen Anne and Romanesque merge.
Above: A recessed arched entrance.
Left: Geometrically patterned railing.

where the solid base of rusticated stone and recessed arches give way to the lighter decorative treatment of shingled gables and decorative woodwork. This type of house has become known as the Annex house, but houses that integrate both styles can be found throughout the province.

Outside the largest centres, the Romanesque houses were a rarity and if the style existed it tended to stand out in the crowd. Stratford's example doesn't seem nearly as imposing as some others. Quantities of arches abound, while decorative stone trim and patterned brick add texture to the façade. The symmetrical balance and the conventional roofline make it less foreboding. The Queen Anne octagonal tower

Arcade of arches — typical Romanesque.

Queen Anne Style

1890-1914

The Queen Anne style or revival is not what its name suggests — a revival of the plain and dignified architecture that characterized the late seventeenth-century reign of England's "Good Queen" Anne, the last Stuart monarch. Rather it has more to do with the excess and eclecticism of another Queen's era — that of Victoria. Not a pure revival like the Gothic or Greek, the Queen Anne drew inspiration and elements from different styles and periods, resulting in buildings that melded a cacophony of towers, turrets, verandahs, porches, gables, and bays into surprisingly light and playful compositions. The picturesque principles of asymmetrical design and romantic spirit that began in the Regency and evolved through the nineteenth century in the Gothic and Italianate styles had become fully integrated into the public's consciousness by the end of the century, and found full expression and unlimited possibilities in the Queen Anne style. While the Victorian age was made up of many styles, it is the Queen Anne that many people refer to as Victorian architecture.

The style was also influenced by a growing reaction to those great heavy Victorian Gothic or baronial "piles" that were built during much of the mid-Victorian period. English Architect Richard Norman Shaw created the Queen Anne out of the "Domestic Revival" or "old English style" pioneered by Phillip Webb in the 1860s. It was based on early English housing of the late medieval, or Tudor, period and emphasized local materials and vernacular details — half-timbering, steeply pitched roofs, cladding, tall chimneys, and moulded brick.

The exuberant Queen Anne produced vibrant, highly decorated houses.

Shaw took this style a step further by fusing elements of seventeenth-century English and Flemish architecture vaguely associated with the late Stuart period, including white painted trim, small-paned windows, balustrades, brick gables and broken pediments with it to create the Queen Anne style. Many in the late nineteenth century regarded the domestic architecture of the late Stuart period as particularly English, a transitional period during which British builders, now well versed in the classical conventions, still felt free to mix in earlier English vernacular architecture, thereby creating something they considered uniquely English. It was a style that met the growing desire to return to (however romanticized) a cozy English domesticity. It was not, however, a revival style, as the elements were freely used and re-interpreted, not copied from archaeology or history texts.

The role of technological change brought on by industrialization should not be underestimated in the evolution of this style. The development of wooden-balloon frame construction freed the structure from the limitations imposed by brick, stone, and even the post and beam, creating the possibility of larger, taller, and more complex buildings. Mass production had reached a point, by the end of the century, where all sorts of inexpensive building materials and trim were available.

The Gamble Geddes house in the Annex neighbourhood of Toronto illustrates the English Queen Anne style. Built in the early 1890s, the house combines the asymmetrical, large, steep gable, tall moulded chimneys, and tile-hung surfaces with the many-paned double-hung windows and classical details such as the consuls that support the projecting gable, as well as the porch, the red brick (including that of the garden wall) and posts with classical stone orbs. The wood trim, originally a crisp white, would provide a sharp contrast to the red brick so favoured by the original Queen Anne builders and the style's nineteenth-century proponents.

For the most part, though, the Queen Anne style that developed in North America was a very different kettle of fish. The style appears to have made its first appearance on this continent shortly before the 1876 American Centennial Exposition at Philadelphia. The British Pavilions at the Exposition were designed in the Queen Anne style and they struck a chord with the American public, who saw in their design an affinity to their own colonial architecture, interest in which was fostered by the celebrations of America's centennial.

Americans added their own colonial motifs to the style, which also became closely linked to the Stick and Shingle styles, two homegrown styles that evolved out of the Gothic revival. The Stick style evolved from the Carpenter's Gothic, which in turn had been heavily influenced by A. J. Downing, whose books promoted picturesque wooden houses and villas based on Gothic, Swiss, and even Japanese influences. The all-frame Stick style (all frame but the chimneys and foundations) emphasized patterned wooden wall surfaces that suggested the structure of the building, following a growing belief in progressive circles that the house's exterior should in some way, even if only symbolically, express its construction.

Red tile, tall chimneys, and classical details reflect the English Queen Anne.

The Shingle style combined the Romanesque and Colonial revivals with the Stick and, later, the Queen Anne styles to form a uniquely American one. Its major defining feature was the way it used shingles almost like a skin to wrap the entire house in a seamless, sometimes undulating surface, which was often left unpainted. Americans preferred the wooden shingles to clay tiles, which they associated with the English. The Shingle style was most popular on the eastern seaboard, where wood shingles had been traditionally used as sheathing since construction in the earliest settlements.

Neither the Stick nor the Shingle style were particularly popular in Ontario but each had its own influence on the Queen Anne style. Also, Stick and Shingle houses tend to be grouped in the Queen Anne category.

The American version of the Queen Anne style was far more ornate than its English counterpart, employing a profusion of turned wood details and trim. The English examples are largely brick, the American wood, following their frame tradition. The Canadian version lies somewhere in between, tending to follow the shape and form of the American Queen Anne but somewhat more restrained in its decoration. The Queen really got going in Ontario during the 1880s.

One interesting Queen Anne house with strong Stick-style

Opposite: A Brockville Queen Anne that owes much to the American Stick style.

associations is in Brockville and is probably as close as one can get to the Stick style in Ontario. It has a typically strong vertical and angular form with square bay windows and tower. Vertical, horizontal, and diagonal boards which are meant to reflect the structure divide the wood cladding. The diagonal cross bracing further enhances the skeletal appearance.

More typical of the Queen Anne style is the Duplessis House in Hamilton, built in 1890. This small frame house has all the Queen Anne trademarks, including the asymmetrical shape with a broad two-bay window ending in a large, steeply pitched gable with decorated verge boards fronting onto the street, and combination clapboard and fish-scale shingle cladding. Glazed and panelled double entrance doors with a transom open onto as large a porch verandah as the narrow site would allow. The verandah has a lacey look; the highly decorative wood trim, including the spindles, slender turned columns, and delicately pierced railing, creates a lively play of sun and shadow on the house's façade. Such intricate woodwork reflects the Eastlake influence. The windows have hooded surrounds.

Above: The Duplessis house in Hamilton, built in 1890.
Top Right: Paired glazed doors with a generous transom create an inviting entrance.
Right: Porch detail.
Far Right: Stained glass and diamond panes add colour and texture.

The treatment of the upper sash on some of the windows, each with one large pane (in this instance made up of a leaded diamond pattern) surrounded by a band of coloured panes, is a common feature of the style.

Similar in character to this house is the residence built in 1898 in Cobourg for civil engineer Henry King

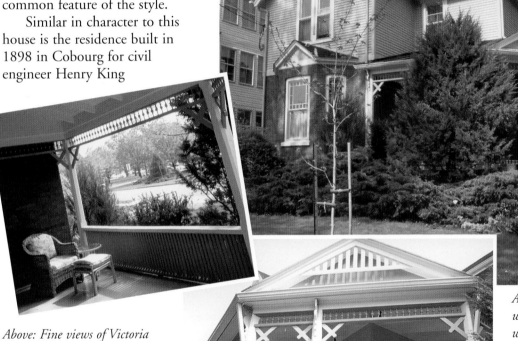

Above: Fine views of Victoria Park from the Wicksteed verandah, Cobourg.
Right: Porch details reflect the Stick style.

Above: Porches and wraparound verandahs were very important to the Queen Anne style. They were extensions of the house and sited to take advantage of the views.

Wicksteed, known for designing yachts. Whether he had anything to do with the design of his house is unknown, but one would presume so. This larger house sits on a more generous lot than the Duplessis House, allowing ample room for a spacious verandah. Not since the Regency had the verandah been so popular. Now, however, its use was unrestrained, as it spread out around the house providing a perfect vehicle for ornamentation. Wicksteed's wraps around two sides of the house and opens at the corner into a pediment. The simple wood cross braces, and decorative elements in the gables show the influence of the Stick style. The form of the house is reminiscent of the Tuscan villa, but without the tower. Three different types of cladding and the brick base, clapboard second floor, and shingled gable are all neatly segregated. The whole house has a tidy, precise character, which suggests the influence of its civil-engineer owner. Located in the gable of the bay window is a stylized sunburst. During the heyday of the Queen Anne style, classical motifs were eschewed for more naturalistic ones. Sunbursts,

Highly decorative woodwork was readily and cheaply available at this time.

Above: A fine example of the Queen Anne style in Waterloo. Inset: Large panes of glass replaced multiple panes around 1870.

sunflowers, hollyhocks, and other flowers were very popular decorations that appeared in wood or terracotta treatments.

The Schiel-Patterson House in Waterloo shares the same basic form as the Wicksteed house, though its decorative treatment is altogether different. Sheathed entirely in buff brick, the house sports a variety of window shapes and sizes, including two round-arched Romanesque-like windows with simply decorated heads.

Except for a modest stained-glass window marking the stairway, all extravagant detail has been reserved for the front porch with its Eastlake decorative trim, turned columns, and classic spindles. The original porch and balcony railings have been replaced. The original contract drawn up by Martin Schiel and local Waterloo builder Charles Kreutziger reveals the organic design process that led to the creation of such houses built by contractors. Among the conditions the contract states that "the house is to be like the Mitchells' in Berlin" (now Kitchener) and the front window was to be similar to the one in a Mrs. Martin's home.

Toward the turn of the century Cy Warman, the

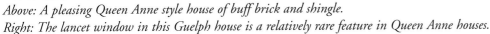

Above: A pleasing Queen Anne style house of buff brick and shingle.
Right: The lancet window in this Guelph house is a relatively rare feature in Queen Anne houses.

author of a love poem that became the lyrics for the song "Sweet Marie," chose to settle with his wife, she of the song, in London, Ontario, the city where they met and where the famous lyrics were written. For their new house, the romantic couple chose to build in the Queen Anne style, possibly influenced by the happy domesticity the style symbolized. Even in fairly modest houses such as this one, complicated roof structures, with broad projecting gables and steeply pitched roofs, were employed to create a fanciful silhouette. In the Warman house the roof dominates the composition. The gables are sheathed in wood shingles that continue slightly below the eaves, onto the flare where they meet the buff brick. This cladding treatment further de-emphasizes the first floor while accentuating the prominence and importance of the roof. Such treatment owes much to the American Shingle style. The ever-present verandah has a pediment denoting the entrance. Small-paned windows are found in the gables. The triple window on the side gable with a shell motif over the middle section, suggests a Palladian window. Warman's name and his sugary-sweet song have passed into near obscurity, but the song's name lives on in the popular chocolate bar named after the ode to his wife — Sweet Marie.

Queen Anne houses were not always the dainty domiciles one imagines, but are often sturdy, particularly when executed in brick, as illustrated here. This 1890s home on London Road West, Guelph, is

Above: Elliptical arches in this Guelph verandah suggest the art nouveau. Right: A porticoed entrance with decorative shingles shelters the entrance.

characterized by strong plain decorative features, smooth stone lintels and sills, a coved eave cornice, and multi-patterned and coloured clay tiles in the broad front gable. The most prominent feature of the house is the large verandah with pedimented entrance. There is no evidence of the spindly Eastlake decorative work here. Strong square posts support a flat roof with a truncated slope containing several rows of multi-coloured tiles. A square projection similar to that of the Wicksteed house pushes out toward the intersection, forming a seating area. The wood shingle balustrade, or skirt, wraps around the entire verandah, while plain,

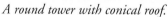

A round tower with conical roof.

The Ryan House, a Queen Anne home in Guelph.

wood arches suggestive of the elliptical art nouveau style span the posts. Turned wood brackets, the incised bargeboards, and leaded and stained-glass windows provide a lighter note. One bit of whimsy is a tiny heart centred in the base of the gable pediment.

Directly across the street in Guelph is the Ryan House, a Queen Anne that borders on the robust. Designed by Toronto architect G. M. Miller, this commanding house is a composition of bays and shingled gables anchored by a large, circular three-storey, vaguely French tower with a tall conical roof. Typical of the Queen Anne, yet like its

Queen Anne Style

A recessed entrance with stone surround.

neighbour, the Ryan house lacks the host of wooden decorative detail one might imagine. The house has some definite Romanesque traits, including the massive masonry walls, rusticated stone details, and the recessed front entrance with stone surround. This was a Queen Anne more concerned with being impressive than invitingly domestic. The house also shows the influence of the Château style, uncommon in houses in Ontario, more than in the United States. It is based on French architecture of the early sixteenth century.

As the popularity of the Queen Anne style waned, elements of the increasingly popular colonial and classical revivals made their appearance in the designs of later Queen Anne houses. This turn-of-the-century brick house in Hamilton has returned to the symmetry of the pre-picturesque period — almost. The tall chimneys, the two-storey projecting side bay with pedimented gable, and the pair of bold circular towers flanking the entrance, however, supply the picturesque. These interesting towers have shingled second storeys and several banding courses which exist at different intervals and correspond to similar courses on the projecting side bay. Interestingly, one band course cuts through the first floor windows, dividing them in two, thereby creating transoms. Centred on the façade and sheltering a modest front door flanked by two windows is a simple, classically influenced, balconied porch. A second-storey doorway corresponding to the first-floor entrance opens out to the balcony and is flanked by two oval windows that correspond to their first-floor counterparts. The multi-paned dormer windows, chimneys, and rich red brick contrasted with crisp white paint are reminiscent of the English Queen Anne as well. One can see from

Above: A transitional Queen Anne house in Hamilton exhibits the growing popularity of classical motifs.
Right: A Georgian-style front door.

this colour scheme what the Geddes House would have looked like with its white painted trim.

While its popularity peaked at the turn of the century, the style continued to be used until about 1910, when the desire for plainer, simpler houses caused the public to choose the foursquare or revival styles reminiscent of English and colonial past. However, the Queen Anne has made a comeback in recent years, as popular suburban track housing revives interest in the elaborate woodwork of the late Victorian age.

The Arts and Crafts Movement

1890-1930

In recent years the Arts and Crafts movement has become very fashionable, not just in its decorative arts fostered by William Morris and his ilk, but increasingly in its architecture. Arts and Crafts, Mission, English Cottage, English Garden, Cotswold Cottage, Bungalow and Craftsman are among the terms used interchangeably to describe the architecture that evolved out of the Arts and Crafts movement. Perhaps because of its recent popularity or its relative closeness to our time, it is still largely ill-defined in the public's mind. Compounding the vagueness surrounding the Arts and Crafts, it was, like the Romantic movement a century earlier, a social movement that captured under its canopy a broad range of ideological and artistic ideas that allowed different paths of expression to evolve.

The Arts and Crafts movement was born in England out of a reaction against industrialization and its negative impact on British society, including what many saw as the dehumanization of people by machines and the decline of art and design wrought by mass-made ornate products. The sorry state of mid-century English art and design was made apparent to some progressives by Prince Albert's impressive 1851 Great Exhibition at the Crystal Palace, an exhibition that was meant to showcase Britain's industrial greatness. John Ruskin, England's greatest art critic of the time, was appalled by the quality of the exhibits and in his influential work *The Stones of Venice*, published in 1851 and 1853, he set out to contrast the machine-made objects of the Exhibition with the craftsmanship of

Wychwood Park in Toronto is filled with Arts and Crafts houses, such as Uplands Cottage, pictured here.

handmade objects from medieval Venice. His views became the tenets of the Arts and Crafts movement: that morality, art, and nature were directly connected and that man's connection with nature came through the act of craftsmanship, from which he had been separated by industrialization. As a result, Ruskin felt a deep affinity to the medieval period. Here the Pre-Raphaelites, a radical group of artists who believed that art since the Renaissance had been corrupted — had lost its connection with nature and therefore its purity — shared his views. The only pure art in their minds, except of course for their own works, existed prior to the Renaissance painter Raphael, hence the group's name.

Yet it was another Pre-Raphaelite associate, William Morris, who founded the Arts and Crafts movement. He took the theories and put them to the test by establishing guilds based on medieval models that created furniture, stained glass, wallpaper, and textiles that united beauty, craftsmanship, and utility. Morris believed that if the quality of the design and the construction method were improved, the character of the individual producing the design would be improved, and, hence, society itself would benefit.

Shortly after his marriage in 1860, Morris commissioned his friend and associate Phillip Webb to design his house. It was thanks to this house, known widely as Red House, that the Arts and Crafts movement found architectural expression. Webb designed a "modern" house, using the informal non-classical English vernacular architecture of medieval times that included tall brick chimneys, brick walls, local materials, and small-paned, often casement, windows. The style has been referred to as English Domestic Revival. It was from this base that Richard N. Shaw developed the Queen Anne style. Not surprisingly, Morris, Webb, and Shaw all worked for a time in the offices of the Gothic revival architect George E. Street. However, Shaw was not as idealistic as Morris and Webb, and his Queen Anne style contained many classical elements that differentiated it from the Morris presentation of Arts and Crafts.

Another group closely linked to Morris and Shaw which had a profound effect on the Arts and Crafts were the Aesthetics, whose reaction to Victorian ugliness developed into a philosophy of art for art's sake, challenging the prevailing attitude that art should reinforce social values by having a moral purpose. Beauty was its own virtue, and by surrounding oneself with beauty, the Aesthetics believed, one enhanced one's quality of life. One of the most famous proponents of Aestheticism was the colourful poet and playwright Oscar Wilde. The Aesthetics valued simplicity and were greatly influenced by Japanese culture and sensibilities after 1854, when Japan opened its doors (or had them forced open) to Westerners. The ensuing late nineteenth-century oriental craze had a profound effect on the Arts and Crafts movement.

The Arts and Crafts style continued to evolve during the late nineteenth century as architects tried to develop a style of architecture – Free style – that was in a sense *devoid* of style, particularly with historical overtones. Yet at the same time they were interested in creating an English style that suggested the traditions of medieval times. Sir Edwin Lutyens, in association with the great nineteenth-century gardener Gertrude Jekyll, produced houses that integrated the Arts and Crafts house with a landscape based on the idealized English Cottage Garden. Jekyll's brother, incidentally, was a friend of writer Robert Louis Stevenson, who probably appropriated the family surname for his famous work *The Strange Case of Dr. Jekyll and Mr. Hyde*. Charles Voysey later developed a streamlined version of these houses, and it was

Above: An intriguing Arts and Crafts house in Gananoque. Inset: The striking three-storey octagonal tower and chimney are central elements of the house.

through this stream that the term English Cottage or English Garden style developed.

In Ontario, the Arts and Crafts movement began to be reflected in buildings in the 1890s and was initially strongly connected with the Queen Anne style and the turn-of-the century Tudor revival. A fantastic example exists in Gananoque. This turn-of-the-century house is a bold statement, with high vertical proportions constructed out of rich red brick with red-shingled gables. The asymmetrical massing, the informal use of the small-paned windows grouped in pairs or in threes, and the lack of decoration is in direct contrast to the ornate decoration characterized by Victorian architecture. The composition suggests, rather than replicates, the medieval. The striking octagonal tower, one side of which forms a triple-flue-chimney, dominates the house and is an indication of the Arts and Crafts's originality.

Some of the finest Arts and Crafts houses in the province exist in Wychwood Park, a small sylvan enclave in the heart of urban Toronto. It was conceived as an artist's colony by Marmaduke Matthews, a prominent British-born painter, as a picturesque residential retreat for his friends and patrons. Naturally, many of the houses built in "The Park" were inspired by the trendy and artistic Arts and Crafts style.

Above: The lopsided, or dipping, gable was an important element of the English Arts and Crafts.
Inset: In pairs or singly, small leaded windows add to the aged feel of the house.

The prominent artists George Reid and his wife, Mary, were among the first artists to move to the park. In 1905, they built Uplands Cottage. Designed by Reid himself, the elegantly simple house was heavily influenced by the work of Charles Voysey's English Cottage style. The horizontal house is long and low, with banks of leaded casement windows, exposed timbers, and irregular and exaggerated roofline. The large, lopsided "dipping gable" and the stucco are Voysey

English cottage-style dwellings were designed around garden courts.

Top: Riverdale Courts, an early, progressive affordable housing complex in Toronto.
Above: Cheerful entrances lead to "cottage flats."

trademarks. Voysey brought stucco into vogue once again having been inspired by a similarly clad Regency house he once lived in.

Another resident of Wychwood Park was architect Eden Smith, who did much to popularize the style in Ontario. His houses became the staple of many Toronto neighbourhoods well into the 1920s. One of his more interesting commissions was Riverdale Courts, an affordable housing project built in 1914, quite progressive for its time. Toronto's rapid growth at the turn of the century created a crisis in low-income housing. Social reformers, philanthropists, and business leaders, under the auspices of the Toronto Housing Authority, commissioned Smith to build a 204-unit complex in the solidly middle-class Riverdale neighbourhood. Riverdale Courts was designed around garden courts in the English Cottage style and incorporated steeply pitched and irregular rooflines, stucco and brick surfaces, half-timbering, gables, bay windows, and porches, all elements found in Smith's tonier projects. The intent was to avoid an institutional character while creating a community or country village atmosphere of cozy domesticity that blended into the surrounding neighbourhood. The units, referred to as "cottage flats," balanced domestic privacy with communal living. All ground-floor flats had stoops that opened onto gardens, while the second-floor units had spacious balconies or porches opening onto the shared gardens. Today that same sense of community continues at Riverdale Courts, which is now known as The Bain Co-op.

One of the guiding principles of the Arts and Crafts architecture was the relationship of the building to its site. Nowhere has that been more effectively developed than at the Fullerton House in Cobourg, which is

Its position being so close to the street only enhances the cottage feel of this delightful Arts-and-Crafts Cobourg house.

located at the end of a quiet residential street, on a relatively narrow but long site that gently slopes down to Lake Ontario. The two-storey stucco house is positioned at the extreme north end of the property with its west façade set toward the street, indeed almost abutting the sidewalk. A charming yet modest front porch with sidelights and door typical of the Arts and Crafts, the casement windows, steeply pitched roof, and irregular massing create the effect of a modest, idealized English village house. One almost expects to see a small front garden full of hollyhocks, lilies, and foxglove surrounding the entrance. From the front of the house one would never guess it was the residence of a well-to-do manufacturer.

Yet the relationship of the house to the site changes dramatically by turning the corner to the south face. Instead of a back–front oriented house, the house is oriented front–side so that its garden face can take full advantage of the lake. The south façade reveals the true, substantial character of the house, as it opens into a long, low structure that extends almost the entire depth of the property. With a broad shingle gable, stucco walls, an unusually recessed porch, and banks of casement windows, the house looks out over an expansive lawn toward Lake Ontario.

Above: The garden front overlooks Lake Ontario.
Right: An attractive, unpretentious Arts-and-Crafts entrance porch.

In the United States, the Arts and Crafts style developed quite differently, yet this variation too had a major effect on buildings in Ontario. The Arts and Crafts style first made its appearance south of the border in the early 1870s, when William Morris's decorative arts products became widely available. However, it wasn't until 1882, when the "Apostle of Aestheticism," Oscar Wilde, made his successful tour of the States, touting Morris and Ruskin and the Arts and Crafts movement, that its popularity grew. In America, proponents of the movement focused on craftsmanship and the use and expression of regional materials. The allusions to an idealized medieval way of life that were so much a part of the English experience did not resonate strongly in the new republic. The English Cottage style, sometimes referred to as the Cotswold Cottage style, was never as popular as it was in Ontario. However, it has been said that three indigenous regional American styles emerged out of the Arts and Crafts: the Shingle style associated with the Queen Anne, Frank Lloyd Wright's Prairie school, and the Craftsman style. The Shingle and Prairie styles never achieved widespread

popularity in Ontario, unlike the Craftsman.

Architect brothers Charles Sumner and Henry Mather Greene are credited with developing the Arts and Craft style in California during the 1890s. They drew from a number of sources, including the shingle and board buildings of California, Japanese and Swiss wooden structures, and the Anglo-Indian bungalow, to create exquisitely crafted informal houses that tended toward the horizontal and used natural rustic materials, large low-pitched roofs with gables, sleeping porches, and banks of windows.

In 1901, New York furniture designer Gustav Stickley began publishing *The Craftsman*, a magazine devoted to promoting to the style of that name. Stickley, the most recognized name in American Arts and Crafts furniture, like the Greenes became interested in the Arts and Crafts after a trip to England. He turned his attention to producing furniture based on honesty and simplicity, emphasizing structure over details and using largely quarter-sawn oak that maximized the wood's grain to achieve his distinctive style. Although Stickley called it Craftsman furniture, in the public's mind it became Mission furniture. How it got this name is up for debate. Some believe the name derived from the Craftsman furniture designed for the 1894 Swedenborgian Mission in San Francisco. Others believe the term came about from the philosophy of the movement or its "mission," while still others suggest the term originated as a result of the influence of the early Spanish missions in the southwest. Whatever its origins, the name has also been applied somewhat incorrectly to the Craftsman architecture. Architecturally, the Mission style is a specific style based on the re-interpretation of the adobe houses built for early Spanish missionaries in the southwestern United States.

While the Craftsman style was used for larger houses, often with two storeys, the more modest one- or one-and-a-half-storey "California" or "Craftsman" bungalow caught the public's imagination and spread throughout North America. Named after the low, hip-roofed Anglo-Indian house that influenced its form, the Craftsman bungalow style provided small functional houses of good quality that were easy to build, charming, and cheap. Low ground-hugging structures which emphasized the rustic textures of their materials, they appealed particularly to the growing number of individuals and families which could now afford a house for the first time. Their simple, open plans met the changing needs of the twentieth-century nuclear family.

While not as common in eastern Ontario, the Craftsman bungalow became a staple in Toronto, where it blended with the English Cottage style, and in western Ontario as well. It first made its appearance in the province in the early twentieth century and by the 1920s whole streets were built in the style.

Cambridge has many larger, handsome examples such as this stucco house typical of the style. The whole of this one-and-half-storey house is contained under a broad gable roof that extends over and includes the spacious front porch. Typical decorative features are the central gable, triangular brackets under the very broad eaves, and exposed rafter ends. The casement windows, small square bay, and front door with its six small panes are typical of the Craftsman features. The texture of the stucco and brick are deliberately rough, while the massive brick enclosed porch

Above: The Craftsman bungalow, an American version of the Arts and Crafts, here sheathed with very British half timbering and stucco.
Inset: Stuccoed piers support the verandah. Pier supports were often tapered.

balustrade melds the building to the site. Its closeness to the low-hanging roof reinforces the house's connection to its site.

The use of stucco, brick, and the half-timbering decoration are Ontario or Canadian adaptations to the style. This form was very popular not just for single-family houses but also for semi-detached ones.

In Cobourg, where only a dozen or so bungalows exist, this frame example shines. Though given a simple treatment, the distinctive Craftsman trademarks are evident in the low-pitched roof, banks of windows, rustic materials, and decorative structural elements. A large front gable projects from the house, carrying forward in part to form the entrance porch that rests on squared posts supported by cobblestone bases. The low-pitch roof has extremely wide overhangs that are supported by bold triangular brackets. The cobblestone chimney adds that extra bit of rusticity to this asymmetrical house.

The use of textured and rustic materials is certainly evident in the Reitzel House in Waterloo. Not surprisingly the owner's family were well-known area builders. The bungalow is clad in contrasting cut-fieldstone and

Above: Broad overhangs, knee-braced brackets, and rustic chimneys are standard bungalow components.
Top right: A neat and attractive Arts and Crafts bungalow in Cobourg.

The rustic character of this Waterloo bungalow is evident in the use of materials and earth tones.

wood siding with a number of shingle-faced gables. The broad overhanging eaves contain decorative rafter tails. The architect has cleverly made the front and side gable low to distract the eye from the steep pitch of the main roof that enables him to subtly fit in a second storey. The Craftsman character is further enhanced by the natural colour of the wood siding. The flat roof of the entrance porch is rather unique.

Builders often adapted the Arts and Crafts to other popular Ontario forms. One popular house applied Arts and Crafts details to a four–square house plan. It provided more space than the more modest bungalow but fitted the smaller urban lots of newly developing neighbourhoods. A good example is this Herkimer Street house in Hamilton. The asymmetrical plan with an off-centre door is made more so by the use of overlapping front gables containing half-timbering. A porch, with half-timbered pediment, extends the length of the façade and is supported by massive piers. The windows, flared bargeboard, exposed rafter ends, and doorway with six-paned window reflect the Arts and Crafts influence.

The popularity of this movement waned after the 1920s.

Top: A stylized gable window.
Above: Rough stone walls form an open porch.

Above: The partially glazed door creates an informal cottage feel.
Top right: American Craftsman reworked for an Ontario audience.
Inset: Arts and Crafts stained glass.

However, the Craftsman bungalow continued to be popular up until the Second World War, when the period revival styles reigned supreme.

Edwardian Classicism

1900-1930

While the return to classical models is often associated with the turn-of-the-century reign of Edward VII, the return to classical architecture began in the late nineteenth century, a decade or more before the sun finally set on Queen Victoria's long reign. A reaction against Victorian high society and tastes spurred new intellectual and artistic thought. In architecture there were two main, and opposing streams, that developed out of this growing disaffection: the Arts and Crafts and the return to the classical. The Gothic no longer adequately expressed England's confident nationalism, based on its overwhelming wealth and imperial greatness. Architects like Richard Norman Shaw turned to the classical baroque, the architecture of the late eighteenth century — particularly the architecture of Wren and Hawksmore — presented a uniquely English style, to reflect England's view of itself architecturally.

In Europe, a similar revival in classical forms was underway but in reaction to the flowery art nouveau style. The École des Beaux-Arts, France's leading art school during the 1800s, had always maintained a formal classical tradition. The Beaux-Arts classicism was less about a revival of the classical and more about a re-interpretation by combining elements of the Greek, Roman and Renaissance to invent a modern architecture suitable for the twentieth century. It promoted functionalism with ornamentation.

Out of a sense of nationalism, in England the French Beaux-Arts

Edwardian Classical house with handsome details including the wide verandah that extends the length of the façade.

classicism was at first eschewed in favour of the English baroque. However, the rigidity of the latter led to adoption of the former in England during the first decade of the twentieth century.

In the United States, Americans embraced the École des Beaux-Arts toward the end of the nineteenth century. Richard Morris Hunt and Henry Hobson Richardson were the first Americans in a long and steady stream to attend the school, for whom a similar reaction against the Victorian occurred. The 1876 American Centennial sparked an interest in American history, particularly in the colonial period, and nationalism surged. The Americans were inclined toward classical architecture which they associated with American nationalism and ideals. The Beaux-Arts style was dramatically presented to the American public at the 1893 Chicago World Fair celebrating the 400th anniversary of the discovery of America by Columbus. Known as the Columbian Exposition, its theme celebrated the classical world. The magnificent, richly decorated classical pavilions provided an optimistic vision that had an immediate impact on Americans. The same style was used again in 1901 for the Buffalo Pan American Fair. The English baroque and Beaux-Arts classical revival styles were particularly suited to grand and formal public buildings and private residences.

As in most cases, Ontario's architecture was influenced by both American and English versions of the style. The Beaux-Arts was extensively used for grand architectural statements, largely public buildings, banks, and schools. A few Beaux-Arts–influenced houses were built, particularly where Americans could be found.

Cobourg at the turn of the century was nicknamed "the Newport of

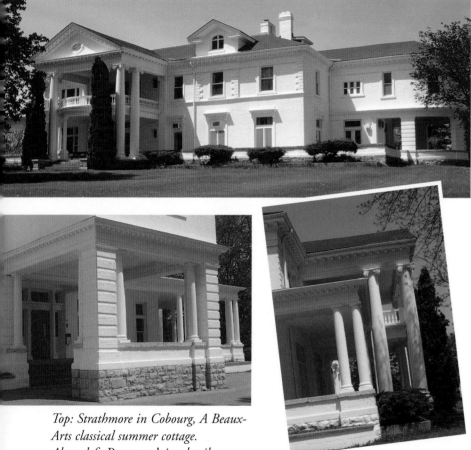

enough to house a spacious upper balcony, dominates the large rambling brick house whose plan has more to do with function than classical symmetry. However, classical details abound in the balustrades, porch columns, quoins, window hoods supported by consuls, and the cornice entablature with square blocks (called modillions or muntins) lining the eaves. Its splendid doorcase, with Ionic columns and pilasters supporting an entablature, in turn supporting four short pilasters and a second entablature, illustrates the turn-of-the-century habit of further compartmentalizing the doorcase by dividing the transom into three windows corresponding to the door and sidelights. Combining function and beauty while emphasizing classical decoration, this impressive cottage exudes the confidence and optimism of the American elite prior to the First World War. Unfortunately for the Donnelly family, their luck ran out sooner. Less than ten years after Charles Donnelly died in 1904, the family was bankrupt and forced to vacate Strathmore with only a few of their personal possessions.

In terms of most residential buildings in Ontario, a much simpler version of the classical house, containing many English and some Beaux-Arts influences, became widespread. Known as Edwardian classicism, it became one of the most popular building styles in Ontario for several decades after the turn of the century.

In a residential area overlooking Cambridge that must rank as one of the most beautiful neighbourhoods in Ontario, several interesting Edwardian classical houses exist, including this handsome and restrained example. Typical of the style is the symmetrical square house with

Top: Strathmore in Cobourg, A Beaux-Arts classical summer cottage.
Above left: Porte cochére detail.
Above right: Porches and porticoes.
Far right: Edwardian beauty, Cambridge.

the North" because of its reputation as a fashionable summer resort for affluent Americans. Several built large summer homes in the Beaux-Arts style. Strathmore was remodelled for one of Pittsburgh's richest men, Charles Donnelly, in 1903. The monumental Ionic portico, deep

Above: A central projection, or frontispiece, was often used in symmetrical Edwardian houses. In this Waterloo example, the projection rises above the roofline and incorporates the central dormer.
Right: The entrance portico forms part of the wraparound verandah.

the front door and upper centre window divided into six segments. Nestled into its landscape well back from the street, the house has a simple and dignified yet substantial presence.

The Snyder-Seagram House in Waterloo is a more elaborate version. The house had all the characteristics of the Cambridge house but adds bay windows, a substantial front porch, asymmetrical wrap-around verandah, and second-floor Palladian windows. Characteristic of the style, too, are the many bevelled, leaded-glass windows. Built for Herbert Snyder, the builder was none other than the town engineer, Charles Moogk, whose professional background may have influenced

hipped roof and centred dormer, tall balanced chimneys, and projecting frontispiece. The commodious porch supported by classically-inspired columns runs the length of the façade. The windows are generous, with

The projecting shingled gable commands attention.

Front-gabled Edwardian houses fit neatly on narrow city lots.

Leaded windows on front door.

Three columns support portico.

the decision to construct the house in poured concrete, a very modern method at the time.

Not all of the Edwardian classical houses conformed to the square, hipped-roof version. Another form, perhaps a holdover from the currently popular Queen Anne style, was often used. This example in Hamilton is a gable-roofed house, positioned with its large end gable — reminiscent of the large Queen Anne gable — fronting the street. The decorative handling of houses such as this vary widely, but they are usually brick, contain a shingled gable, bay windows, double-hung windows, bevelled-glass front door, and a large front porch. More expensive details – rusticated stone trim, some added classical motifs, and a broad front doorcase – make this example a cut above most others.

A much simpler form or a stripped-down version of the Edwardian classical house developed to meet the needs of those with more modest means. It also shared a stylistic connection

The simpler brick foursquare was once an Ontario standard.

Short Tuscan columns on brick piers were common Edwardian porch features.

Column detail.

porch, off-centre doorway, and dormer window. This Guelph house is representative of the thousands built throughout Ontario. In the United States, they were mostly clad in clapboard and shingle, but the tradition of building in brick ensured that most in this province were so sheathed. The popularity of this house was reinforced by pattern books and plans and pre-cut houses that could be ordered from catalogues, such as Sears Roebuck, and shipped all over North America. Eaton's Canada followed suit, developing their own versions of plans and kits to meet domestic needs.

One such house may be St. Andrew's Rectory in Grimsby. The house follows the standard Edwardian classical symmetrical design, with hipped roof, dormers, and pedimented porch, double-hung one-over-one sash windows, wide eaves with modillions, or simple brackets, and bay windows. However, the brick base contrasting with the clapboard upper floor is unusual in Ontario and suggest an influence from the United States, where contrasting sidings were popular, an Arts and Crafts influence. The spacious asymmetrical wrap-around verandah is

with the Queen Anne and Arts and Crafts designs. In the United States, this house was known as the American Four-square, two rooms wide and two rooms deep. The cube shape made most of the limited space; it was practical, easy to build, and fit easily on a small lot. In spite of its modest cost it was an attractive house whose appeal depended on its shape and proportions, not its decoration. Typically it had two storeys with a wide-eaved hipped roof, front

Generous verandahs continued to be popular well into the twentieth century.

Hexagonal paned windows were popular around 1910.

oriented to look toward the church and is particularly inviting. One can envision many a pleasant church social on the grounds of this gracious old rectory.

Edwardian classicism continued as a popular housing

This gracious Grimsby Anglican rectory shows both Edwardian classical and Craftsman styling.

form into the 1930s. It eventually gave way to new forms of housing which were more suited to the growing suburbs, where the nuclear families colonizing them demanded houses with a sense of space and openness. Its high styles, particularly the Beaux-Arts classicism that

sought to create a modern twentieth-century architecture through classical idioms eventually withered and died out, as attention turned to the progressives, who advanced the modernists' manifesto, "form follows function," and adopted the international style for a truly modern age.

Revival Styles

1890-1930

At the turn of the twentieth century a dramatic shift in taste in residential architecture occurred as the public embraced a new set of revival styles. Georgian, Tudor, and colonial revival styles were among the most commonly employed, but their popularity signified much more than a change of fashion. It signified a change of attitude.

In 1901, the Victorian age came symbolically to an end with the quiet death of England's longest reigning monarch. For over sixty-three years England's diminutive powerhouse, Queen Victoria, presided over an age of unparalleled political, social, and economic change in England, Europe, and North America. So long was her reign that many couldn't remember a time before it. And such was her impact and longevity that her name became synonymous, not only in the British Empire but in the United States, with this tumultuous period of rapid urbanization, industrialization, and technological advancement.

Yet by the time of her death many had begun to believe modern life was too complex and moving far too rapidly for comfort. A nostalgia for simpler, more traditional times developed as people yearned for order and stability in their domestic lives. This conservative backlash led many tastemakers back to the era prior to eighteen-year-old Victoria's ascension, the Georgian age of proportion, simplicity, and chaste good taste. Ironically, it was the reaction to this period's architecture and taste that had caused the first round of architectural revivalism in the early nineteenth century.

Steep roof and low ground floor suggest thatched Tudor cottage.

Today we tend to think of the Victorians as stuffy and conventional. However, the Arts and Crafts, Queen Anne, and even the Edwardian classicism were creative attempts to evolve a modern architecture from historical precedents. The turn-of-the-century revivalists turned their backs on modernism, preferring the familiar security of historical copyism.

Ironically, the early twentieth century revivalism developed from those same creative nineteenth century artistic innovations. In the late nineteenth century, interest in classical motifs was revived by Richard Norman Shaw's Queen Anne style houses, and the reassessment of the architecture of Christopher Wren led to a style of architecture (known later as Edwardian classicism) that freely interpreted English architecture of the 1600s and 1700s. Out of this latter movement sprang a group of architects who sought a more disciplined interpretation of the Georgian style by recreating the proportions and detail of Georgian architecture. Many felt that the neo-Georgian was not just a return to traditionalism but to good taste. Many Edwardian tastemakers considered Victorian art and architecture vulgar. They believed the Arts and Crafts movement was a transitional period necessary to lead everyone back to the good taste of the Georgians.

Around this time Americans rekindled an interest in their own colonial architecture, though not so much from a desire to return to good taste but from a historical nostalgia springing from the successful 1876 centenary celebrations. The American Centennial renewed in the American people a pride and sense of national accomplishment. Its colonial period, previously considered rather primitive, was now revered — found

Above: Georgian elegance revived in the early twentieth century.
Right: Classically detailed porch.

worthy of scholarly study and celebration. Historical societies sprang up around the country and families scrambled to discover a Mayflower ancestor. National monuments such as Washington's famous home, Mount Vernon, were preserved and enshrined. Colonial architecture had first found its way into the Queen Anne style by replacing the British motifs of Shaw. Later, as interest in colonial times solidified, a few wealthy Americans began to build country houses in the style. In large measure, colonial revival style was based on the English Georgian colonial architecture of the Thirteen Colonies. By the beginning of the twentieth century, its simple sense and dignity, like that of the English neo-Georgian, appealed to the public's growing desire on both sides of the Atlantic for a simpler, more ordered life, in contrast to the "free for all" of the Victorian age.

The revolution in housing design was only one part of the revolution in domestic living. Just as the Edwardian generation reacted against Victorian excess in the arts, they revolted against the rigid, rule-ridden life of the respectable Victorian. North American daily life, in particular, was streamlined and simplified as formal manners eased. Technology played a major role in the revolution. By the 1920s most houses had electricity, central heating, plumbing, and a variety of new appliances such as refrigerators and washing machines. Such innovations and the skyrocketing cost of domestic help reduced the need and desire for large houses with complicated floor plans. Most of the middle-class revival houses were being built without a servant's room, a feature no self-respecting Victorian would dare omit, even if the prospect of being able to fill it was remote. Home owners, particularly women, wanted efficient, practical, and easy-to-run houses.

Social life became less focused on the individual home, as recreational organizations, such as country clubs or tennis clubs and, later, restaurants and nightclubs became centres of socializing and leisure. At the same time, home ownership became a symbol of success for the middle classes. The idea of owning your own little bit of country sprang from the House and Garden movement that idealized informal country living. It is by no means a coincidence that the magazine *House and Garden* began publication in 1913 just as car and commuter trains allowed many to realize this romantic dream in the suburbs.

With its associations to idealized colonial times and the good taste of the Georgians, the informal simplicity and restrained elegance of the revival houses with their efficient floor plans and landscaped gardens perfectly suited the conservative values of tradition and stability and the aspirations of lineage and legitimacy.

Always influenced by the British and Americans, Ontario too had matured to the point where there was an interest and pride in its early

Cornice detail, Hamilton.

history. Organizations such as the Ontario Historical Society were started, while the United Empire Loyalists became Ontario's counterpart to the Pilgrims, and many early historic figures such as Laura Secord and General Sir Isaac Brock were venerated. A number of Ontario architects attempted to incorporate early Ontario motifs into their revival buildings, but for the most part, the revival houses here would seem not out of place in the United States or even Britain.

Hamilton's surviving rich architectural heritage belies its steel-town reputation. For over a century, "the ambitious city" was a major industrial centre and the affluence it produced can be seen in the attractive residential districts that survive. Southwest Hamilton, one of the city's toniest sections, contains many impressive colonial and Georgian revival houses, such as this 1920s Undercliffe Street example. The solidly rectangular house is symmetrical, with central hall plan, hipped roof, and balanced dormer windows and chimneys. Revival houses tend to be bigger and exaggerate the details, such as in this house's decorative dentiled (tooth-like) cornice, and flat window arches with prominent keystones over the six-over-one double-hung sash windows. The projecting front entrance with its bold entablature and plain columns is more reminiscent of the Greek revival, while the flat-roofed form surmounted with a elegant metal balustrade is rather contemporary in design, as is the snappy decoration in the chimney heads. The two small windows balanced above the entrance, where one would expect a window identical to the others, is a nod to the modern conveniences contained within.

A much earlier example of colonial revival exists in the historic town of Grimsby. This 1905 handsome transitional house illustrates the free use of colonial and Edwardian classical elements. The three-bay symmetrical

Early classical revival house — Grimsby.

house with gable end roof, returning eaves, and a dentiled cornice is colonial-inspired. The exaggerated, pedimented portico with paired columns and the blind recessed arches containing the ground floor windows are neo-classical, while the stuccoed cladding suggests the Regency. Yet the house's chunky proportions and the front portico's roomy porch-like size evoke the Edwardian. Added into the mix are some leaded casement windows tucked under the eaves. The overall result is of a very attractive turn-of-the-century revival house.

Turn-of-the-century version of a neo-classic porch.

Many later revival houses were built with closer attention to historical accuracy than the Grimsby example, to the point that a modern observer might indeed believe them to be early houses. This Guelph Georgian copy proudly proclaims its construction date, 1928, on its elegant rainwater heads. Such handsome houses were derided by the modernists as copyist, but for charm and livability few can beat them. The six-panelled door with semi-circular transom is contained in a pedimented door supported on columns. The side porch with treillage is a twentieth-century touch. There is very little difference between the British Georgian and American colonial revival house. Neo-Georgian houses, it can be argued, are larger and more detailed. However, clapboard siding is one telling difference. While colonial revival houses are sometimes brick, English neo-Georgian houses are never clapboard. In Ontario, brick was the overwhelmingly popular siding

Top: A classic Georgian revival house.
Above: Rainwater head proclaims the house's construction date.

Above: The treillaged porch – a 1920's touch.
Left: A convincing copy of a Georgian doorcase.

material for revival houses. Toward the mid-century the use of clapboard increased.

Homewood in Port Hope is an early example of a clapboard colonial revival house, although it is now stuccoed. At the turn of the

century Port Hope attracted a number of summer residents, a spillover from neighbouring Cobourg's bustling resort. The James Schwartz family from Pittsburgh began summering in Port Hope shortly after the turn of the century. Homewood was built by one of his sons in 1904 opposite his father's summer house, Hillcrest. Sitting high on one of Port Hope's many picturesque hills, the solid blockish colonial cottage with steeply pitched roof, pedimented dormers, massive plain chimneys, and a

Above: The Colonial revival was at first very popular for country and summer houses. Homewood, in Port Hope, is an example.

Left: A turn-of-the-century interpretation of a Palladian window.

large front verandah has a commanding view of Lake Ontario. The house is largely symmetrical, except for the window and door treatment of the façade's first floor, which contains an arrangement of paired windows, a simple unadorned wide front door, and a modified Palladian window, all characteristic of the turn of the century. All the exterior details, including the eave cornice, door and windows surrounds, and verandah with Tuscan columns, are very plainly treated. The original clapboard was painted deep mustard-yellow, a more historically correct early eastern-seaboard colonial house colour. Later owners stuccoed the house. Its present crisp white look is reminiscent of George Washington's Mount Vernon. For a number of summers Homewood was occupied by Frank Schwartz (the son of Hillcrest's James Schwartz) and family. Frank later anglicized the family name to Black during the First World War. Frank's wife, Leila, found the proximity to her mother-in-law too close and the family eventually took a summer house in Cobourg, a comfortable distance away.

Colonial North America was made up of many different ethnic and regionally based colonies that developed their own cultural and architectural traditions. As the penchant for colonial revivalism developed, more and more of these early regional colonial styles were revived. Other than the classically inspired styles of the Thirteen Colonies only a few made it into Ontario. The Spanish colonial, based on the Mission buildings and houses of the southwest, influenced the province's architecture later in the century. However, the Dutch colonial appeared in Ontario before the First World War.

The defining feature of the Dutch colonial is its gambrel roof. The gambrel is a curbed roof with a steep double pitch, the lower pitch being steeper and sometimes with a flared eave that gives the impression of being rounded. This roof, combined with typical colonial revival

A spacious London Tudor revival with half-timbering and tall, plain chimneys.

The gambrel roof has come to define the Dutch Colonial revival.

elements, defined the Dutch colonial. The McClelland house in Niagara-on-the-Lake is an excellent example. Like many Dutch colonials, the gable end of the long narrow clapboard house faces the street and projects over the front porch running the width of the house. The gambrel roof is one and a half storeys in height. A prominent roof-ridge moulding exists where the pitch changes, and forms returns, which

create the appearance of upper roof pediments at the gables. A similar side gambrel gable is found on the east wall of the house. The origins of the gambrel roof are vague. The term "Dutch colonial" suggests it came from the Netherlands, but no such roof structure exists there. It was, however, widely used by both English and Dutch settlers in New York State, particularly in the Hudson Valley area and in New Jersey, all part of the former Dutch New Netherland colony. Prior to its use in revival houses, the gambrel, probably because of its colonial origins, was used extensively on nineteenth century Shingle style houses. Other elements of the house, including the porch details, simple eave cornice, pediments, dormers, and windows, are all typical colonial revival.

Classically inspired revival houses weren't the only historical knock-offs on the block. Tudor revival became increasingly popular in the early 1900s. Its antecedents were the houses of the late English Reformation period from the Tudors to the early Stuarts. The style is also known as Elizabethan (after the last Tudor, Elizabeth I) or Jacobean (after the first Stuart King, James I). Tudor revival developed in the late nineteenth century. Much of the Gothic revival, even for residential design had its origins in ecclesiastical architecture, not domestic. Richard Norman Shaw

Front entrance, London.

and others started to design large manor houses based on the sixteenth-century domestic buildings rather than religious ones. Manor houses represented the power of the English gentry and the lifestyle of country gentlemen, powerful associations to upwardly-mobile twentieth-century middle-class businessmen. In the first decades of the twentieth century, Tudor revival houses, sometimes known derisively as "stockbroker Tudor," "Tudorbethan," or "Jacobethan," began to appear alongside their Colonial revival counterparts. One of the most defining characteristics of the style was the use of half-timbering, a decorative element mimicking the structural timber frame of Elizabethan houses. The space between the timbers was "nogged" or filled in with stone, brick, or more often, stucco.

The Tudor revival and the Arts and Crafts movement were closely related and shared many characteristics, evident in this early Tudor revival house, built in 1913 for Charles Keene, a prosperous businessman. One obvious Tudor revival characteristic is the abundant use of vertical half-timbering which covers the entire second floor. Arts and Crafts houses often used this as a decorative feature in gables or on bay windows. In the Keene House, the first floor is brick. This manner of using half-timbering with a contrasting base of brick or stucco was common to Tudor Revival houses. The asymmetrical Keene house is less consciously cottage-like or picturesque as it tries to more accurately depict a Tudor-era house form. Still, the house retains a strong sense of the Craftsman style, with its bargeboard, exposed rafters, front dormer, and entranceway.

The manorial-looking house on Aberdeen Street in Hamilton is representative of the mature Tudor revival style, although it contains no half-timbering. The two-and-a-half-storey rectangular house is rough

Above: A rough stone Tudor revival, Hamilton.
Right: Two-storey bay with casement windows.

stone with a steeply pitched gable end roof with eaves tight to the walls. The arrangement of the different architectural elements on the façade gives it its casual asymmetrical arrangement. Instead of a chimney on each gable end, there is only one. It helps to balance the broad off-centre parapet, with a moulded stone finishing course, or coping, located off-centre on the façade. To the parapet's left is the porchless Tudor arched doorway (with vertical plank door), and hood mould, typically not a major feature in the composition. Porches are very rare in Tudor revival houses. Occasionally, the entrance is recessed into the house. The banks of leaded casement

Above: A steeply pitched half-timbered gable.

Right: A quaint English-style cottage.

windows, capped by hood mould, are surrounded by stone trim that contains small tabs of stone projecting into the brick and resembling quoins. The stone sills are canted, or cut, to slope away from the window. This expensive treatment is reserved only for the windows on the façade. A square, leaded bay window and a pair of Georgian-like windows round out the façade design.

Westdale, a unique residential community where fine Tudor-revival houses line its pleasant streets, was an example of progressive urban planning when it was developed in the 1920s. Its plan was inspired by the Garden City movement, a turn-of-the-century British urban planning philosophy that advocated planned, self-sufficient, and limited-size communities combining the benefits of town and country. The Garden City movement was the forerunner of modern urban planning. Although not as self-contained as some of the English models such as Letchworth, Westdale's residential areas radiate from a limited commercial area forming the centre of the community. In some ways, garden cities were intended to be ideal English villages. Certainly this was the intent of Westdale where most of the early houses were Arts and Crafts-inspired or Tudor revival. The latter soon supplanted the former in popularity. However, in the last stages of development, colonial revival houses appeared, thereby reducing the area's "olde English" feel. Most of the Tudor revival houses are similar to the Aberdeen Street house and are modelled regardless of size on Tudor manor houses.

An interesting and atypical Tudor revival house exists on Oak Knoll. When McMaster University located in Hamilton on the edge of Westdale, many professors moved into the neighbourhood, fostering the belief that it would become a "colony of professors." This Oak Knoll house was built by one such British professor who brought the plans for his new Canadian house with him when he immigrated. Unlike its neighbours, this house is based, not on Tudor manor houses, but on Elizabethan thatched cottages. A large, steeply-pitched hipped roof dominates the house. Its eaves extend low, reducing the height of the brick first floor and thus enhancing the home's cottage-like character. The façade is informally asymmetrical, the massive roof broken by a sharp, upright half-timbered gable that turns neatly into a shed dormer containing a bank of casement windows. The façade is further embellished with a large projecting square bay, a dormer window, and a Tudor revival vertical-plank front door flanked by sidelights. The living-room bay window is a later addition, and although quite sympathetic, it diminishes the architect's intent to downplay the first floor. This surprisingly large house was very much planned as a three-dimensional composition and is nicely sited on its corner lot to give full expression to its cottage form.